MONTEREY
PUBLIC LIBRARY

THE MAN WHO COULD READ STONES

THE MAN WHO COULD READ STONES

Champollion and the Rosetta Stone

By ALAN HONOUR

ILLUSTRATED BY ANTHONY AVILES

Hawthorn Books, Inc.   **Publishers**   *New York*

Δ
921
C 4535 h

First Edition, April, 1966

5645

For Joe Longstreth
a good friend and counsellor

AUTHOR'S NOTE

In telling the story of the astounding accomplishment to which Jean-François Champollion dedicated his life, I have also tried to give a picture of his times. This remarkable man spent a lifetime of devoted effort in deciphering the hieroglyphics, rediscovering for mankind the civilization of ancient Egypt. Even though his own world heaved and thrashed like a wounded animal, despite the ridicule, mockery and bitter criticism he suffered for his ideas, he worked quietly toward his goal. The courage, endurance and faith of Jean-François Champollion brought him to the pinnacle of fame. The triumph of his quest, a truly inspiring tale, led to the firm establishment of the science of Egyptology.

It has been said that, while the revolution which gave birth to the United States of America succeeded, the French Revolution which closely followed failed. The point scarcely tolerates scrutiny, for the struggles for freedom, the ideas and the furies which created these two revolutions continue. This is true not only in France and the United States of America; injustices similar to those which culminated in revolution in these two countries now divide the whole world in bitter ideological struggles.

In a sense, however, the French Revolution was an immediate failure, for after a decade of bitter struggles for power the Republic dream was shattered; and the stage was set for Napoleon Bonaparte and military dictatorship.

Napoleon restored many lost privileges of the Church and nobility over which much blood had been shed. Yet, in serving himself, Napoleon also served France and mankind. Napoleon's imagination, his belief that he could be a second Alexander the Great, opened up the Middle East, the treasure house of man's ancient history that had been lost for centuries. Adventurers, diplomats, curious men of all kinds followed the route of Napoleon's military conquest of Egypt. Napoleon's path to empire revealed the riches of ancient Egypt to scholars of the caliber of Jean-François Champollion.

Although based upon facts and true incidents, the conversations employed in this book are largely imaginary. The author would like to acknowledge his great indebtedness to Miss Renate Miner of New York City for her invaluable assistance in translating from the German.

Thanks are also due to my friend Mrs. Elinor P. Zaki of New York City and Mrs. Dora Neuman of Richmond, Indiana, for their kind help. The author also wishes to express his gratitude to the staff of the Morrisson-Reeves Public Library, Richmond, Indiana, for their unfailing aid in tracking down obscure information.

ALAN HONOUR

CONTENTS

CHAPTER 1

JACQUOU THE MAGICIAN

Monsieur Jacques Champollion sat with his elbows on the edge of the table in the room behind his bookshop, his hands pressed to his head. A doctor had just left the house.

It was the early summer of 1790, but the narrow streets were cool, for the sun did not bathe them except part of the day. The barnlike house, capped with a wavy, red-tile roof, stood a few yards off the Place des Armes in Figeac, southwest France. The front of the house was cut in the middle by a wide door and four staring windows, two at ground level and two above.

As the doctor left, twelve-year-old Jean-Jacques Champollion came into the room, crossed to his father and put his arm around his shoulders. Although it was summer the house was draughty, and the only heat came from large, open fireplaces.

"Will Maman get better?" Jean-Jacques asked his father.

Monsieur Champollion looked up at his son and sighed. "*Mon fils*, the doctor offered no more hope than they did at the sanitarium where she has been. He could give me nothing that would ease her pain or make the swelling of her joints go down. It is hopeless."

Blinking back the threat of tears, Jean-Jacques crept up-stairs to see his mother. Madame Champollion was unable to walk, for the fearful swelling in her ankles and knees and arms made it impossible for her even to leave her bed. She dozed fitfully, moaning in pain now and then as she moved in the big brass bed. Jean-Jacques sat quietly watching her.

Jeanne Françoise Gaulieu Champollion was a well-loved wife and mother. Her suffering filled the old house with gloomy foreboding.

Figeac is situated on the right bank of the river Salle in the Department of Lot. On three sides it is enclosed by vine-covered hills which form a natural amphitheater. It lies about midway between the Bay of Biscay and the Mediter-ranean Sea. Though Figeac was the chief town of the dis-trict, there was little about it that was notable. It was a typi-cal, small rural center in the agrarian France of 1790. Even then there remained a feudal atmosphere about the town of five thousand inhabitants. Figeac had grown up around a Benedictine abbey which was founded by Pepin the Short in A.D. 755. Wine, linen and cotton manufactures, along with cattle-breeding, formed the basis of the economy. De-spite the activity of its business life, Figeac had an air of torpor about it.

South and west of the town were two *aiguilles*, octagonal obelisks over fifty feet tall that had been built in medieval times. In the feudal period, at night, fires used to be lit on top of them as a measure of public safety and a guide for travelers approaching the town.

In 1770, on the advice of an uncle, Monsieur Champollion had moved to Figeac from the province of Dauphine. He had prospered and now owned the house in which he lived. Once the house had been quite a grand establishment and Monsieur Champollion was trying hard to repair and restore it to its original condition, but it was a hard task and he constantly fought the dampness. He wondered sometimes if the damp and draughtiness was the cause of his wife's illness. As he thought about his troubles, a sudden alertness caused Monsieur Champollion to rise from his chair. The situation called for a magician; he was convinced of it.

The majority of the people of Figeac were Roman Catholic and they were ardent in their religion, but at the close of the eighteenth century, as Madame Champollion lay desperately ill, there was still a widespread belief in the power of magic. No doubt this, and the many superstitions adhered to by the people, had been carried over from the Middle Ages. There were still practitioners of magic and sellers of charms well known and respected for their skills.

Jean-Jacques heard his father's soft call and went down the stairs.

"I have made a decision," Monsieur Champollion said in a determined voice. "Since the doctors offer us no encouragement, you must run an errand. Hurry to the house of the magician, Jacquou. Tell him your mother is ill and cannot leave her bed. Tell him the doctors have abandoned her case. Urge him to come and see me at once."

Jean-Jacques stared at his father in surprise. His father

was an intelligent man and did not generally hold with superstition and magic.

Seeing his son's face, Monsieur Champollion said with some exasperation, "It is all we can now do. We must try it! Things will not be the worse for our having tried."

Jean-Jacques raced off to the house of Jacquou. The magician, with due respect for the town's bookseller, returned with the boy immediately.

"I have consulted every doctor within reach," Monsieur Champollion told the magician. "They all say they cannot discover the cause of my wife's illness. She eats nothing and cannot even leave her bed."

"Bah!" said Jacquou. "Those doctors are pompous charlatans! They cannot even agree among themselves on a simple diagnosis. Drawing blood from the sick is their 'cure' for everything! Where is your wife?"

There was some justice in Jacquou's comment, for the practice of formal medicine was still a somewhat crude affair in 1790.

Monsieur Champollion led the magician up the narrow stairs to his wife's sickroom. Jean-Jacques followed and stood fidgeting at the door.

Jacquou placed a rough peasant hand on the woman's forehead and felt her swollen wrists. He stood, immobile, gazing fixedly at the stricken woman for several solemn minutes, then suddenly lifted her hand and carefully studied the palm.

Jacquou, who had a cunning knowledge of the medicinal properties of certain herbs, turned sharply to Monsieur Champollion. "Your wife's case is not hopeless," he said, and in low rapid speech, he gave strange instructions to the wondering bookseller. "You must gather a large quantity of herbs and mix them together in a brew. The milky juice of dandelions is a good medicine and digitalis will stimulate your wife's heart. Cook gentian roots, for these will help her regain an appetite, and add houseleek, for it is a good pain reliever. Eyebright will clear the stuffiness from her head. Rhubarb is valuable, too, for it mends disorders of the stomach."

Jacquou continued his unusual list. Valerian he recommended for its antispasmodic properties and he emphatically stressed the disinfectant value of rue, an herb long used in practices of magic and medicine. For aroma he included kitchen herbs such as rosemary, marjoram and lavender. "Heat these herbs over the fire," he instructed. "When they are still warm, pack them about your wife's body on the pallet of her bed. See to it, also, that she consumes large quantities of hot wine, for this will warm her blood and help drive out her pains."

The magician turned to Madame Champollion, who was now awake and listening intently. She felt no alarm as she looked into the glittering dark eyes of the weather-roughened face. On the contrary, Jacquou's look filled her with new hope, for she saw no malevolence in the magician.

"Have no fear," Jacquou said to her gently. "You will soon be well." Noticing Jean-Jacques in the doorway, he lowered his voice. "*You are carrying a son in your womb. This boy will become very famous, and his fame will survive through centuries to come!*"

Madame Champollion's eyes glistened with tears, and she

felt hopeful for the first time since she took to her sickbed. Jacques Champollion was skeptical, for his wife Jeanne was forty-three. They had long ceased to expect the blessing of more children. Nevertheless, he was very grateful to Jacquou as he paid him for the consultation.

Monsieur Champollion, with the help of a neighbor woman, wasted no time in carrying out the magician's suggestions, and for several days the house was fragrant with the heady aroma of pungent herbs and steaming wine.

Three days after the strange visit, Madame Champollion left her bed. Her swollen joints were almost normal again. "It is a miracle," she cried, "a miracle! I am free of pain at last!"

Seven months later, at two o'clock in the morning of December 23, 1790, Madame Champollion gave birth to her second son, Jean-François Champollion. *Jacquou's prediction of the birth of a son had come true,* but the joy of the Champollion family was tinged with apprehension.

"The child seems strange," Jacques Champollion said to his wife a few days later.

"Strange? How?" Madame asked.

"Look at his eyes." Monsieur Champollion pointed. "The corneas are yellow! He has the eyes of an oriental! His hair is so dark, and his skin too!" He peered more closely at his smiling, wide-awake son. "Do you suppose Jacquou's magic has had this influence?"

She had to admit that her baby's eyes had a definite upward tilt at their outside corners, and that the child's complexion was unusually dark. Madame Champollion looked at her child, then hugged him close to her breast. "Faugh!"

she exclaimed. "I am sure there is nothing to fear from Jacquou. Maybe the yellow eyes will mean that the baby will be able to see in the dark!" She chuckled. "Jacquou is a kind man. He said I would get well, and so I did. He said I would have this child, and I have! And remember what else he said? Perhaps that, too, will come true, and the boy will grow up to be famous." Remonstrating with her husband, she laughed aloud. "Do not worry, Jacques, everything Jacquou told us was of good to come, not evil. Anyway"—she rocked the child in her arms—"he is a beautiful boy and seems so happy and content. I do not intend to worry simply because my baby *looks* different from others."

Thus the matter was left, for Jacques Champollion was content that all was well with his wife and the new son. Jacquou might well be right with the rest of his prediction. After all, his older son, Jean-Jacques, had already proved himself to be exceptionally bright in his studies. The thought reminded the bookseller he would have to be giving attention to his older son's further education. Figeac could not offer the facilities for the learning he wanted for his sons.

The Champollion home was a happy one and Jean-Jacques was delighted with his baby brother. He felt very protective toward the child and played with him whenever he could. Soon he began to call him "Cadet" (junior). The affectionate nickname stayed with Jean-François for many years.

Perhaps because he grew up with the love his much older brother lavished upon him, or perhaps there was another reason, but Jean-François preferred older people

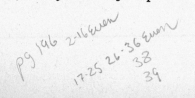

17

about him rather than companions of his own age. There seemed always to be somebody near to pay attention to him. Gaily, Jean-Jacques would skip home from school and, entering the house, would call for his brother, whom he knew always played hide-and-seek when Jean-Jacques was due home. "Cadet," Jean-Jacques would call, *"Cadet, où es tu?"* (where are you?). Finding him, Jean-Jacques would lift his brother high into the air, saying, *"Comment ça va, mon petit chou?"* (How's my little cabbage?).

"Be careful with François," Madame Champollion warned gently, happy to see her sons so close to one another. These were great days for Jean-François, surrounded as he was with such attention.

CHAPTER **2**

THE OLD REGIME

These were great days for France, too, great and terrible, for the France into which Jean-François was born was in the throes of change. No one could be sure of what the future would hold. The year 1790 was, in a sense, the first year of the revolution—the revolution against the Old Regime.

The France of the Old Regime was essentially a feudal society divided into three estates, or orders. Everyone belonged legally to an estate and was bound to it. At the head was the king, who ruled by "divine right." This meant that his authority, which in theory was absolute, came from God and not through the will of the people. After the king, the First Estate was the clergy. The Church was the biggest landowner, and over 130,000 persons belonged to this estate, managing its vast affairs. The Church added to its coffers by demanding tithes on the agricultural produce of the realm. The Second Estate in this order of society was the aristocracy, consisting of about 150,000 persons. Some of these were connected with the king's opulent court at Versailles and basked in royal privileges. Others lived in the provinces. But whether or not these nobles were absentee landlords or concerned proprietors of their lands, all added to the burden of the peasant by exacting dues, taxes and fees of myriad kinds.

The Third Estate was made up of everyone else in France, over nine-tenths of the population. Four-fifths of these were farmers and peasants, for France was almost completely an agrarian society. The rest were the growing bourgeoisie, or townspeople, the merchants, shopkeepers, factory owners and professional men. The most miserable peasant in France and the most learned lawyer, the richest businessman and the poor but educated bookseller like Monsieur Champollion all belonged to the same order of society. Though certain members of the Third Estate had great economic power, they had practically no political or legal rights. The king could dispense money and favors at will, make laws, declare war, seize property of any citizen and have him put into jail.

Despite the authoritarian control centered in the person of the king, the structure of government was very loose. France was a collection of large provinces divided into many semiautonomous divisions which carried out the king's orders. Jurisdictions overlapped, there was no system of law, tariff boundaries differed and provincial feeling ran strong.

So it was on the eve of the French Revolution: over 90 percent of the people of France paid taxes to the king, dues to the lord, and tithes to the Church, equalling about 80 percent of their income. They knew no equality of status or opportunity, and privileges divided them from each other even within the same estate. There was no real liberty of any kind—no religious liberty, no civil liberty and no political liberty.

The winds of change were fanned by philosophers skeptical of the old ways who believed in Reason individually exercised. Montesquieu, Voltaire, Rousseau and others violently criticized the regime and clamored for liberty in all spheres. Montesquieu, in his *Spirit of the Laws*, advocated a constitutional monarchy, the power of the king to be checked by the legislature and the judicial branch. Voltaire, with his fiery pen, satirized abuses of individual liberty and religious bigotry. Rousseau, in his *Social Contract*, championed political equality for all and the sovereignty of the people. So were the causes of the revolution exposed and passions inflamed by intellectuals of France.

The revolution was precipitated by a financial crisis. Large and small wars had drained the treasury, and 5 percent of the annual expenditure went to support the king and his court. By 1787 France was on the verge of ruin. No one was willing to lend money to the state and successive treasurers had failed to find a solution. The Parlement, or tribunal, of Paris demanded the calling of the Estates-General, asserting that no taxes could be levied unless those that would have to pay them agreed to pay them. On May 5, 1789, for the first time in 175 years, the Estates-General was called. Though the Third Estate was allowed double membership, the assembly still met as it had in centuries past— each estate sat separately and voted by order and not as individuals.

The issue was resolved dramatically when the Third

Estate, realizing it would still be at the mercy of the First and Second Estates, who could outvote it, broke away and declared itself a National Assembly. In the famous Tennis Court Oath, made when its members were barred from their meeting place, they swore "never to separate, and to reassemble wherever circumstances shall require until the constitution of the kingdom shall be established." A week later, by the command of the king, all three estates met together and the National Assembly, or Constituent Assembly, as it called itself, was complete.

The days that followed were punctuated by outbreaks against the Old Regime. Aware of the king's distrust of the Assembly, mobs stormed the Bastille in Paris, a symbol of royal tyranny. A new government was formed for Paris, on an elective basis. Throughout the land, as far south as the province of Limousin, where the Champollions lived, the peasants, who had already suffered from the poor harvests of that year, burned the hated feudal records, even the châteaux that held them.

Then, at the National Assembly on the night of August 4, occurred an extraordinary event in the history of nations. The nobles and clergy relinquished their privileges, class distinctions were abolished and equality established as the basis of society and the state. Shortly after, hungry for bread, and fearing the king might endanger their new-found liberties, for he had not ratified the decrees of August 4, crowds of Parisians forced their way into Versailles and brought the king and his queen to the Tuileries, the royal palace in Paris.

At the end of August the DECLARATION OF THE RIGHTS OF

MAN was proclaimed, which embodied the principles of liberty, equality and brotherhood—*liberté, égalité et fraternité*—the rallying cry of the revolution. The people were declared sovereign and the law the expression of their will.

The Constituent Assembly gave way to the Legislative Assembly, which framed a government, a constitutional monarchy, but the constitution of 1791 was not ideal. The legislature was elected only indirectly by the voters and the state was still in dire need of funds. The lands of the Church were declared national property, but this failed to settle the financial problem. The Civil Constitution of the Clergy was established to bring the clergy and their incomes under state control. The clergy were now to be elected by the citizenry and not appointed within the Church.

Needless to say, this rash move split not only the clergy but the people of France into two groups, and put all conscientious Catholics, including the king himself, in an impossible situation vis-à-vis the revolution. In June, 1791, the king and his queen, Marie Antoinette, made an unsuccessful attempt to escape to allies across the French-Prussian border.

Meanwhile, to add to the tumult of the times, two political clubs were growing in power and vied for control of the Assembly. These were the Jacobin Club, led by Robespierre, and the Cordelier Club, of which Danton and Marat were members. These clubs, which debated the issues before the Assembly, represented a vociferous element in the revolution and their influence was great. The Jacobins grew more and more revolutionary in character and allied themselves with similar clubs all over the country. By 1793 they boasted a membership of half a million people.

There was another liberal political group within the Assembly. The Girondistes were intellectuals and visionaries who, in the years to come, would be caught in a death struggle with the Jacobins. It would be the Jacobins who would rule France through the dreaded Commune during the Reign of Terror. But in 1791 the Girondistes held sway over the more conservative members of the Assembly. Their influence took France into a war with Prussia and Austria, countries which stood with Louis XVI and the old order against all that the revolution hoped to accomplish.

The war was going badly. The king vetoed two decrees of the Assembly—one to deport priests who defended the Civil Constitution, the other to provide 20,000 men to protect Paris against the Austrian enemy. Incensed by a manifesto issued by the leader of the armies of Austria and Prussia that threatened the revolution and the city of Paris, in June, 1792, the mobs stormed the Assembly, then forced their way into the Tuileries. By this time the Jacobins had established their own government, the Revolutionary Commune, which engineered the insurrection. The snarling mobs discovered the king in his apartments. As Louis XVI faced them, they handed him the red cap of the revolution with its red, white and blue cockade. Looking sheepish, the king took the cap and put it on his head. This humiliation of their king mollified the mob and there was no violence that day.

Two months later the king was not so lucky. This time the mob tore into the Tuileries and created a havoc of destruction in its glittering interior. Tapestries were ripped from the walls. Screaming harridans rushed in and out of the elegant rooms, with fine clothes stolen from court ladies draped over their rags. The Commune dictated the overthrow of Louis XVI and Marie Antoinette and had them imprisoned along with thousands of their nobles. During the bloody days before a new convention was called to draw up a constitution for the Republic, the rats of Paris grew fat and bold on the corpses lying in the streets, adding the fear of plague to the half-crazed mobs. News of French reverses in the fighting with Prussia and Austria drove the mobs to even greater frenzy against anyone who seemed to threaten the revolution. News in September of a French victory at Valmy, on the border of eastern France, placated the mobs for a time.

One of the first acts of the National Convention was to sentence King Louis XVI and Marie Antoinette to death. They went to the guillotine early in 1793. The Jacobins had made their move for power in the National Convention against the more moderate Girondistes. So confident were the Jacobins ruling the National Convention that they declared their intention of annexing Belgium and Savoy, and decreed their guarantee of democracy to the peoples France would liberate. The only result of this piece of diplomatic clumsiness was to create new enemies for France and further alarm the rest of Europe. Now, to consolidate their power by suppressing all opposition, and to create a strong government for France, the Jacobins established a Grand Committee for Public Safety, which, in reality, administered the whole country. Maximilien Marie Isidore de Robespierre emerged as leader of the Jacobins and acted as Public Accuser. A new national militarism (there were

770,000 under arms) swept the country and the Reign of Terror began. An estimated 5,000 "enemies of state" were slaughtered during this period from the summer of 1793 to the summer of 1794.

The terror spread to the provinces. The shouting of the mobs bent on vengeance, the raucous singing of revolutionary songs, the screams of the victims, penetrated the old house just off the square in Figeac. Three-year-old Jean-François, wide-eyed, watched the refugees who slipped into his father's house, seeking aid and shelter. Monsieur Champollion did what he could, but he had to take care that he did not attract the attention of the mobs and bring their anger down upon himself and his family.

Two Benedictine monks, who would not swear to uphold the Civil Constitution of the Clergy, were among those Monsieur Champollion sheltered during the Reign of Terror. In gratitude, Pere Seycy of Nice undertook to tutor Jean-Jacques, but by the time Jean-François was old enough to begin his education, Seycy was a very sick man. Canon Dom Calmet then became tutor to young Jean-François. The sensitive little boy responded to everything he saw and heard. Dom Calmet soon noted that, young as he was, this child had remarkable intellectual powers. He was astonished at how quickly the boy grasped, and seemed to retain, everything he was taught.

Monsieur Champollion was not a wealthy man, but he made a comfortable living for his family from the bookshop, and their house was an island of culture in bucolic Figeac. Thus, from the beginning, Jean-François was exposed daily to books and learning. He was never forbidden to listen to the conversations of adults and the family was a happy one, considering the daily tumult beyond their house. Jean-François's brother, fourteen-year-old Jean-Jacques, was deeply infected by the cries of the revolution, the struggle for liberty and a decent way of life for the people. Some boys his age actually took part in the street fighting, roving in gangs singing the "Marseillaise." This song, written in 1792 by an army officer, Rouget de l'Isle, was called "The War Song of the Rhine Army." The revolutionaries seized upon this lilting hymn of freedom and it became the "Marseillaise," giving the mobs something to provide the illusion of a unity of purpose.

For Jean-Jacques, a very intelligent youth, a great, new, shining France of the people was coming into being. Soon there would be no more tyranny, no more poverty and misery. Bloodshed would end and an age of accomplishment would follow.

The horrors perpetrated during his growing years were to teach Jean-François many lessons about the dark side of man's nature. He was to learn the power of the petty and small to torment greatness. He was to witness the terror and corruption of tyranny. On more than one occasion he was to suffer at the hands of men, torn by greed and envy and maliciousness.

Five years before Jean-François was born, an event took place in Paris which, unknown to any of the parties concerned, was to play a vital part in the lives of the Champollion boys. In 1785, Napoleon Buonaparte graduated from the Military School in Paris with the rank of Second

Lieutenant of Artillery. Napoleon was of Italian descent, a native of the island of Corsica, off the south coast of France. He dropped the Italian "u" from his name, Gaullicizing it to Bonaparte. Napoleon, thus far a man of little distinction, and very poor, saw his opportunity. He sided with the revolutionaries against the royalists. Though the Bourbon court, in exile, was active, Napoleon saw little likelihood that they would ever again sit upon the French throne.

In the wave of national militancy the time was ripe for Napoleon. Youth and daring would supplant the old and traditional in warfare. Gradually a group of brilliant young generals rose within the ranks to lead the forces of victory. Napoleon would be the most brilliant of all.

CHAPTER **3**

BOY OF THE REVOLUTION

At first, Jean-François was too young to understand the meaning behind the Red Terror, but the struggles did not end before he had grown up sufficiently to understand. In his home there was much talk and discussion of the rights and wrongs of the republicans and the royalists. For all the pity and sympathy one might feel, there could be no denying that the royalists themselves were responsible for much of their present misery.

By July 1794, Marat, Danton and Robespierre were dead, the massacres had diminished and the revolution was officially declared over. But there was little peace for France. Uprising still followed uprising in Paris. The nation was trapped in a tangle of unrest with no party powerful enough to hold the government together for long. The ill-defined urge to liberty, loosed by the first uprising against the king, remained strong. Harvests had been better, attention was given to reforms in the educational system, but the treasury remained depleted.

Torn within, the country continued to wage foreign wars in an effort to increase its power and influence in the world.

France wanted its place in the sun, its share of the world, which was being carved up into colonial empires. The modern states of Germany and Italy had not yet been born. France struggled with Austria, Sardinia and Prussia. England, with a wary eye on Russia, tried to maintain a balance of power, making sure that none of these ambitious states grew too strong or powerful enough to dominate all Europe. Alliances could change, treaties could be broken overnight. Enemies and friends switched sides alarmingly, each seeking the greatest advantage for its aims.

Ambitious, but cautious as yet, Napoleon had risen to the rank of Brigadier of Artillery. This promotion was his reward for his part in the seige of Toulon. This key port on the south coast of France was vital to France's position in the Mediterranean. The royalists, in the name of young Louis XVII, had turned the port of Toulon over to the English. A combined Spanish-British fleet was riding anchor in Toulon harbor. By skillful placement and use of his guns, Napoleon blew them out of the harbor in December 1793, and returned Toulon to the government in Paris. Serving with Napoleon at Toulon was Paul Barras, who took due note of Napoleon's skill. This notice, later, was to be of great significance for France.

For a while after this, Napoleon idled in Paris with no specific command, but he hated inactivity and feared he might pass into obscurity. He had no desire to relinquish the position and prestige he had gained. Once, near despair, he commented to a fellow officer, "There is no opportunity for advancement in the service of France, it seems. Perhaps I should offer myself in the service of the sultan of Turkey?

There seems to be plenty of activity in Asia Minor." Had he followed this course, history would have been very different. Wisely, Napoleon refrained from becoming identified with any of the individuals or parties struggling for control of France. Napoleon trod a path between the struggling Jacobins and Girondistes, taking care to avoid involvement with either group.

Jean-Jacques Champollion had a warm attachment toward his brother from the young boy's birth. Now, aged fifteen, Jean-Jacques was, most of the time, away at school in Grenoble, about 160 miles east of Figeac, and though there was much to interest and entertain little Jean-François in the bookshop, he looked forward to his brother's visits home. Then he could listen to stories of the big world beyond Figeac. He enjoyed his daily walks with Dom Calmet, but it was not long before Dom Calmet realized and admitted that it was beyond his powers to cope with the young boy's insatiable curiosity.

Fortunately, Jean-Jacques was very patient. Constantly his brother brought him newly discovered books for explanation. Jean-Jacques was amazed that his brother seemed drawn to anything he found from the classic periods of Greece and Rome. Nor did it escape Jean-Jacques's notice that Jean-François seemed not to care much about the great soldiers of those periods. Rather, Jean-François eagerly questioned his brother about the great thinkers and philosophers of the periods.

The word philosophy caught Jean-François's imagination. "What does that word mean?" he asked.

31

"*Philo* is a Greek term originally," Jean-Jacques replied. "It means love." He explained some of the many words that begin with *philo*. "Philadelphia, for example, means brotherly love. Philosophy itself is believed to have been coined by Socrates sometime during the fifth century B.C.," he went on. "Socrates made up the word to describe his love of, and the search for, wisdom. Philosophy describes a system that furnishes a rational explanation of the nature of reality." Jean-Jacques went on to describe other words that derived from the term, such as philosophic and philosophize, and how these words differed in meaning.

"Show me how to write the word, Jacques," Jean-François pleaded.

A little staggered that his young brother had so swiftly grasped what had just been explained, Jean-Jacques reached for pen and paper and printed the word philosophy and the others he'd explained to his brother.

Most young people struggle when they first begin to wield a pen or pencil; Jean-François held his pen as though he were long accustomed to using it. Jean-Jacques supposed that this was because he had spent so many hours absorbed in scribbling on paper. The letters were just a little bit shaky, but perfectly readable.

"Well," said Jean-Jacques, "that's very good indeed! How would you like me to show you the whole alphabet?"

"I would love that," Jean-François replied excitedly.

For the next few hours Jean-Jacques sat with his brother going over the alphabet and the sounds of the letters the young boy was now efficiently copying. The next day Jean-Jacques was even more surprised to find his brother's dark

head bent over the table in the bookshop with several sheets of carefully copied letters and words they had discussed the day before. The young lad had committed them all to memory.

Within the National Convention, a man needed to be nimble if he was to maintain his place or rise to power. Some men were revolted by the excesses of the Reign of Terror as conducted by Robespierre's Committee of Public Safety. The leader of one of the power-seeking groups within the National Convention was Paul Barras. Robespierre hated Barras for his dissolute habits and he feared his boldness. Robespierre tried to get the name of Barras on one of his lists of those marked for execution.

Barras was well aware of Robespierre's hatred. Unscrupulous Paul Barras began his career as a distinguished actor. He served twice with his regiment in India. He could be prudent and he was a good speaker, but there was little else that was admirable about him. Alert to the whisperings and shufflings that were a regular part of the business conducted in the convention, Barras knew that his enmity with Robespierre was reaching a climax.

Like many others who clung to the stricken body of France, Barras was a ruthless, self-seeking scoundrel of the worst sort. Though he served the revolution, Barras was a noble by birth. He had squandered his inheritance in profligate living, and by siding with the Republic he saw a means to recoup his fortunes. Nobleman though he was, Barras did not hesitate to vote for the execution of the king. In Paris, all too often yesterday's friends became tomorrow's enemies.

Finally, Barras maneuvered the Assembly to the point where its members wanted the blood of Robespierre. There was no mercy for the once strong politician who had sent so many others to their deaths. He was led to the guillotine in the Place de la Révolution (now the Place de la Concorde). It was July 1794. Barras emerged a virtual dictator, as general in chief of the army, but only for a short while.

After the bloody Reign of Terror, the inevitable reaction set in. The influence of the Parisian proletariat declined and that of the more conservative bourgeoisie increased. The republican constitution of 1792 was, in fact, never put into effect, but a new constitution was framed by the Assembly which entrusted legislative power to two chambers chosen by indirect and somewhat restricted election. The lower house of 500 members proposed laws and a Council of Ancients, 250 in number, examined the legislation and enacted it. The executive power was vested in a committee of five Directors who were to be elected by the legislature. This Directory, as they were called, appointed other executives, the ministers of state and the cabinet, and they supervised the enforcement of the laws.

It was the end of the year in Figeac. Jean-François Champollion was just four years old, a handsome, very serious young boy, easily excitable, who had an air of wisdom about him that belied his years. His thick dark hair, deep-biscuit-colored skin and oriental eyes alive with intelligence, caused him to stand out. He was quite at ease with older people, but with other young people he was withdrawn. He seemed to have no desire to play with boys his own age and even the activities of older boys bored him. Adults were startled at his self-assured manner and the ease with which he conversed, though some remarked that the boy was extremely nervous and high strung. Most people were drawn to him and indulged him, but the boy seemed happiest pondering the things he discovered in books. Already, though barely four years old, he had taught himself to read!

The young bookworm had done this by making lists of words he knew by heart, then breaking them up and comparing them to the whole written words, reading them aloud over and over again. Needless to say, his brother was delighted with this feat. Sometimes poor Dom Calmet thought his head would burst under the steady barrage of questions from Jean-François. Dom Calmet simply did not have the background to tell the boy the things he wanted to know.

At Grenoble, sixteen-year-old Jean-Jacques had already gained a fine reputation as a skilled philologist and Greek scholar. Despite the differences in age, the Champollion brothers were close companions. Whenever Jean-Jacques was in Figeac, the boys spent hours talking together and young Jean-François absorbed, like blotting paper, the information his brother fed him. His seemingly insatiable desire for knowledge pleased Jean-Jacques immensely, but he also realized that in Figeac the boy was not making the progress he was capable of making.

Discussing Jean-François with his father one day, Jean-Jacques made some acute observations:

"There is an indefinable quality of mind in Cadet and I believe he will go far in the world. Oh, I know I gave him some assistance, Father, but really, once he grasped the principle of taking words apart, then putting them together again, he taught himself to read! Cadet is going to need special attention in his schooling."

"I am well aware the boy is different," Monsieur Champollion said. "Just what this extra something is that the boy possesses I cannot tell. Perhaps it is a gift from God? Anyway, Jacques, Cadet isn't yet five years old. It is too soon to make decisions. Dom Calmet does all he can to guide him."

Jean-Jacques paced the room agitatedly. "There are students much older at Grenoble who are not as quick to grasp things. François should not be measured by ordinary standards," he continued. "He absorbs things, makes them his own, then plunges on to something else he finds more interesting. It may appear that his mind wanders but this is not the case."

Monsieur Champollion shrugged his shoulders in characteristic fashion, holding his arms outspread. "But Jacques, who is there in this small town for the boy to go to? François is too young to go to school in Grenoble. Let us wait a while, then we shall see. In the meantime, I do what I can and he is helping himself learn. He is always with his head in a book and I do not forbid him any book he picks up in the shop."

And thus matters rested.

In 1795, the paths of the Champollion boys and Napoleon drew a little nearer. There was an uprising in Paris against the Convention. The mobs took to the streets, and carts were thrown across the roads as barricades. Cobblestones were ripped from the pavements for use as weapons against the cavalry. Some men armed themselves with clubs, muskets, some had pikes, anything to strike back at the troops.

The Convention had to be protected against this insurrection by bourgeoisie and royalist sympathizers. Calling upon the general-in-chief of the army, Paul Barras, the Convention entrusted him with the task of organizing his forces to disperse the rebels.

Napoleon was at a low point in his career, fretting over lack of action, when Barras summoned him. "Well, Bonaparte," Barras greeted him, "the barricades are up again and I want you to knock them down! I am giving you an army of five thousand troops. I don't care what methods you employ. Break up the barricades, disperse the mobs. Get me results and get them quickly. You should have no trouble, with the guns and troops I am holding ready for your command. Remember," he added with an undertone of threat, "so long as I control the Army, all will go well for us."

Napoleon was quick to realize what such an opportunity to serve Barras could mean to him. He also knew that, in these mad times, Barras could easily be toppled. Still, he could always claim to be just a soldier carrying out the orders of the Convention as given by Barras. He put these thoughts aside, saluted, and accepted the commission.

Napoleon was extremely successful. The outnumbered rebels were no match for his forty commandeered cannon and were quickly routed. Napoleon had his soldiers fire volley after heavy volley of grapeshot into the rabble behind the barricades, who were unable to withstand such concentration of fire. They broke and fled. Their dead and wounded were left to whatever mercy Barras might show.

The insurrection was over. As a reward, Napoleon was made Commander of the Interior. Napoleon was gratified, but he picked his way carefully, still keeping clear of entanglements with politicians. He wore civilian clothes most of the time and sought the company of scientists and artists, writers and other learned men in Paris. From them he learned much about Egypt, and his imagination was fired.

In 1796, his star rising, Napoleon married Vicomtesse Beauharnais. Marie Josèphe Rose had traveled to Paris from her home on the island of Martinique, in the West Indies. Her family had emigrated from France to Martinique many years before and, though not rich, lived the life of nobility in the French colony. Rose, as she was called by her family, went to Paris for an arranged marriage to Vicomte Beauharnais. He treated her with contempt, for her plainness and country mannerisms appeared crude in Paris. But his wife mastered all the arts and graces, learned all the nuances of Parisian society, and improved her looks. She became a beauty and a fine lady in her own right.

Vicomte Beauharnais, for his political intrigues, went to the guillotine. His wife wrote letters to everybody she thought could help, without regard for the fact that her husband had treated her so despicably. She seemed not to realize that she endangered herself. For her trouble she was arrested and learned the fear of the guillotine, but she escaped the final penalty. She was now careful to address herself as Citizeness Beauharnais. Marriage to Napoleon secured her safety. In turn, her connections with men in high places could be useful to Napoleon.

There is no doubt that Napoleon was madly in love with the now beautiful woman from Martinique, as his first love letters to her prove. He had been separated from her only two days after the marriage. Perhaps because he did not want to be reminded of a first husband, or, as some maintained, because of his love for his brother Joseph, Napoleon called his wife Josephine.

Barras, now feeling very secure, had sent once more for Napoleon. This time, Napoleon emerged from the interview with the command of the Army of Italy. Taking a passionate leave of his new wife, he left for the front as head of the Army of Italy.

Inspecting his new command, Napoleon was appalled by what he found. Nevertheless, he also saw his opportunity. "Soldiers," he said to his troops, "you are ill-fed and almost naked; the government owes you much, it can give you nothing. Your patience, the courage which you exhibit in the midst of these crags, are worthy of all admiration; but they bring you no atom of glory; not a ray is reflected upon you. *I* will conduct you into the most fertile plains in the world. Rich provinces, great cities will be in your power; there you will find honor, glory and wealth. Soldiers of Italy, can it be that you will be lacking in courage or perseverance?"

Napoleon's strength fired the badly equipped, poorly led troops with new hope and determination. Unhesitatingly they gave him their loyalty.

French forces had not fared well in the fighting against

40

the Austrians and Sardinians. On April 11, 1796, Napoleon defeated the superior enemy, by dividing them, in a skillfully fought battle at Montenotte, in the mountainous region between France and northern Italy, a few miles from Genoa. Gratified with his successes, "the little corporal," as Napoleon was now affectionately called by his troops, exhorted them to further effort. "Soldiers," he said, "in fifteen days you have won six victories, taken twenty-one stands of colors, fifty-five pieces of cannon, and several fortresses, and conquered the richest part of Piedmont. You have taken fifteen hundred prisoners and killed or wounded ten thousand men. But, soldiers, you have done nothing, since there remains something for you to do. You have still battles to fight, towns to take, rivers to cross."

The next battle, at Lodi, proved beyond doubt Napoleon's skill and his courage. The Austrian forces, opposed to the French, withdrew across the river Adda. The only way for Napoleon to reach his enemy was across the bridge of Lodi. This 350-foot-long bridge was well covered by Austrian cannon. Aware of the murderous fire that his men would face, Napoleon knew that there was no other way but to cross that long bridge. He ordered his grenadiers forward, but halfway across they were reeling under the concentrated fire of the Austrian guns and began to fall back, leaving piles of dead and wounded. Recklessly, with his officers beside him, Napoleon raced to the head of his faltering troops, risking his life each step of the way. His courage inspired his men and, despite the intense fire being rained upon them, they fought their way across the bridge and seized the Austrian batteries.

Reporting to the Directory in Paris on this action, Napoleon said, "Of all the actions in which the soldiers under my command have been engaged, none has equalled the tremendous passage of the bridge of Lodi."

The next target was Milan, after the Sardinians capitulated to him. With the fall of Milan, all northern Italy was open and collapsed before Napoleon. After defeating several armies that were trying to relieve the beseiged city, he captured Mantua. To the consternation of England and the rest of Europe, Napoleon turned against the Papal States. This action was not in his orders from Barras, but he went ahead anyway.

Again Napoleon conquered. Pope Pius VI was forced to cede the papal lands of Avignon, Ferrara and the Romagna. These were taken over by France, and Barras watched his protégé with great interest. One more successful battle was fought in the Tyrol against Austrian Archduke Charles, and Napoleon's victories in command of the Army of Italy were complete. He returned to Paris to find himself a national hero.

Some of the news of Napoleon reached Figeac, but Jean-François learned more when his brother returned home from school. Jean-Jacques was very enthusiastic about Napoleon. He was no doubt influenced in this attitude because the whole city of Grenoble was loud in its expression of joy at the victories of Napoleon, which seemed to foreshadow peace for France.

CHAPTER 4

IT STARTED WITH NAPOLEON

Jean-François Champollion was seven years old when he first heard the magic name Egypt, but a hidden spark in his soul burst into flame. He quivered with excitement, as though he knew somehow that Egypt was to be the very breath of his life. The young lad's eyes reflected the fire in his soul whenever he found someone who would talk to him about Egypt.

Jean-Jacques, now nineteen, looked at Cadet with wonder, almost forgetting the boy was only seven. He talked with Jean-François of how he hoped to teach him classical Greek. But Jean-François wanted most of all to hear about Egypt, especially about ancient Egyptian hieroglyphics. In some indescribable way, it seemed as if the boy was reacting to some instinct.

"Hieroglyphics," Jean-Jacques explained to his brother, "is a term the classic Greeks gave to ancient Egyptian 'picture' inscriptions, but they never learned to understand what the symbols meant. *Hieros* ἱερός means sacred. *Glyphein* γλύφειν means to write or carve. The Greeks," he went on, "did think it might be some kind of writing. They

43

had so profound an awe of written speech that they believed it was a gift to man from the gods. These symbols must, indeed, be very ancient."

Chin resting on his fists, eyes big and round, Jean-François listened. "Few Europeans are bold enough to travel far into Egypt these days," Jean-Jacques said. "Egypt is controlled by the Sublime Porte from Constantinople. The Arabs, especially the desert Beduin, are fierce and cruel. They will murder foreign travelers for the flimsiest of reasons and there is no real authority to control them. Very little is known, really, of any of the lands on the other side of the Mediterranean."

"But what about those strange inscriptions, hieroglyphs you called them? What do you know about them? *Are* they writing of some kind?"

Jean-Jacques grinned. "Nobody really knows for sure what they are. I've heard several different opinions. Some travelers have reported immense temples, pyramids, great structures littered all along the banks of the river Nile. There was Richard Pococke fifty years ago. And only five years ago James Bruce, who is a Scotsman and was British consul at Algiers, published five volumes on Egypt."

"But the hieroglyphs," Jean-François insisted, "they *must* have some meaning, I feel it! The ancient Egyptians wouldn't have covered their temples with them without some reason."

Jean-Jacques was impressed by his young brother's insistent logic. "Well now, Cadet, you must realize that hieroglyphics have not been part of my studies at school. What I know of them I have discovered through my researches

44

into ancient Greece. Some men have tried to study them seriously, but there are so few examples available in France. As far as I can tell, the whole subject of hieroglyphics is smothered in confusion.

"Most of what is known," Jean-Jacques continued, "comes from the classic authors of Greece and Rome, who have written about the peculiar signs of birds, animals, plants and other mythical symbols carved and painted on monuments. Some of the early writers traveled in Egypt long before the last of the Roman emperors. The Old Testament, too, as you know, refers to ancient Egypt. But because there is no proof that the hieroglyphs have a meaning, anyone is free to offer an opinion on them, and that is where the confusion lies."

Jean-Jacques explained that the search to find a meaning in the symbols was usually an attempt to seek an understanding based on their religious significance.

Jean-François read everything he could find, which was then very little, that had to do with ancient Egypt. The subject became a passion with him; he could hardly think of anything else. The discussions with his brother gave him much to ponder.

For some fifteen hundred years, every "modern" scholar, if he pursued the study of hieroglyphics, followed the ideas of the classic writers. These scholars believed that, if the symbols ever had a meaning, it *must* be religious in nature, and was also irrecoverably lost. Some even suggested that the true meaning had been deliberately hidden by Egyptian priests, and in time even the priests had forgotten what the signs meant. The classic writers were heeded, though not always believed, simply because they had lived and worked so much closer in time to the ancient Egyptians.

This was a frustrating and discouraging theory, but Jean-Jacques quickly pointed out to his brother that not all scholars shared this gloomy view. There were some men who believed that the meaning of the symbols *could* be discovered and who worked at the mystery. The "translations" offered by amateurs who had no facts, no evidence to support their ideas, were the despair of the trained minds that did try to solve the problem in a serious manner.

"I know one interesting item," Jean-Jacques said. "There is supposed to be in existence somewhere in the world a study of hieroglyphics written by a man sometime in the fourth century after Christ." He told Jean-François what he knew of this story.

Horapollo was an Egyptian scribe. When he was alive, the meaning of the hieroglyphs had already been lost. All Horapollo could do was wander Egypt, questioning any of his countrymen he thought could help him. Horapollo gathered what scraps of the traditions of the pharaohs still lived on and a few bits of interpretation that remained of some of the hieroglyphs. He put this material into a book.

"As far as I know," Jean-Jacques said, "Horapollo's own work has never been found. There is a purported translation of it that was made by a Greek named Philip who lived two centuries after Horapollo. But I wouldn't doubt that Philip added touches and colorations of his own to whatever original material of Horapollo's he might have had."

There was a solemn look on the dark, handsome face of Jean-François as he asked, "Do you think, when I am grown up, we shall be able to travel to Egypt together? I should like that very much."

Jean-Jacques ruffled his brother's hair and laughed. "If you become famous, as Jacquou predicted you would, it might be possible," he said. "Cadet, do you remember that I told you some of the hieroglyphs are enclosed within a sort of oval?" Jean-François nodded. "Well, a teacher of mine who is now in Paris, Monsieur de Sacy, believes the signs that are enclosed within these cartouches have some special significance. He believes the signs are enclosed in a cartouche for special emphasis, much in the way we underline a word that is to be stressed.

"Another man, Akerblad, who is a well-known Danish scholar, says that *he* thinks some hieroglyphs might very well stand for sounds and could even be letters!"

Jean-Jacques regretted as much as his young brother that these encounters passed so rapidly. He was becoming convinced that Jean-François was going to make a mark on the world. Whatever Jacquou had said must be true. This strange, dark-skinned brother of his was starving for knowledge. Jean-Jacques shared with his brother each new thing about Egypt that he learned from scholars in Grenoble and Paris.

In this same year, 1797, the path of Napoleon drew closer yet to the lives of the Champollions. Napoleon was fully aware that his hold over the Army provided a powerful support for the government and its control over France. Meanwhile, he was nursing a dream—the same dream that had obsessed Alexander the Great. Alexander's path to greatness would be his own.

Napoleon had once, a few years before, known the humiliation of having to pawn his watch in order to eat even in cheap restaurants. Now when he rode out in public he was accompanied by a bodyguard of Polish lancers in glittering uniforms. He had learned much from his association with French men of learning and his conversation reflected his greater knowledge. He was admired and was the topic of discussion everywhere. The sometimes witty, sometimes profound utterances he made were repeated over and over again. His self-assurance had grown enormously. Yet he remained wary, holding his growing arrogance in check.

"What I have done so far is nothing," he said. "I am but at the beginning of the career I am to run. Do you imagine that I have triumphed in Italy in order to advance the lawyers of the Directory? Let the Directory attempt to deprive me of my command and they will see who is the master. The nation must have a head who is rendered illustrious by glory."

Whether such revelations of Napoleon's ambitions were known to him or not, Barras had no intention of depriving Napoleon of his command. Once again Barras had need of his powerful commander.

In its struggles with Britain for the riches of the East and world power, France was seriously considering the idea of an invasion of England. Napoleon knew this, but in his own mind, the idea was impractical; nevertheless, he took command of the Army of England, as the French forces assembled to conquer England were called, and set out on a tour of inspection of the channel ports. What he discovered only served to convince him that the French could not suc-

ceed. To do so they would need to wrest command of the oceans from the British. Such a feat, in Napoleon's view, would not be possible for many years. Nor did he relish the idea of remaining in Paris, once more running the risk of being forgotten after the adulation he had received. Napoleon had tasted glory and he liked it. There was another way to fulfill French aims. Could he, he wondered, convince the government of the worth of his own plan?

Already, Napoleon was building up a clique whose loyalty was to him personally. Two spies he had sent to Malta returned with their report. If he were to act, he must do it now while success was within reach. It was a daring, risky plan, but Napoleon believed that if the British were to be driven out of India, which he believed to be the source of England's power and wealth, and crushed in Europe, it could be accomplished only by following the path of Alexander the Great through Egypt and Persia into India.

The idea of conquering and colonizing Egypt was not original with Napoleon. It had been proposed to Louis XIV by Liebnitz and others years before, but nothing came of the scheme. But there were many Frenchmen who hoped for the day when France could seize the riches of the East.

Eloquently, Napoleon outlined his plan to Barras and his ministers. "With only twenty-five thousand troops I can succeed," he claimed. "There have been no reports of English ships in the Mediterranean. They must know of the plan to invade across the channel so it is to be expected they will keep their ships close to England. At Toulon, our fleet is lying ready to sail."

Napoleon said nothing of the fact that he was beginning to see himself as a second Alexander the Great!

It was agreed that Napoleon should carry out his plan. By 1798, all France was agog with rumors of the coming expedition to Egypt. Incredible elaborations of the scheme were spread by word of mouth.

Jean-Jacques Champollion, who was now a professor of Greek at the University of Grenoble, was thrilled when he heard the news that scientists and scholars of all kinds were to accompany Napoleon. "We are one of the best universities in France," he urged the faculty. "Let me try to secure a place as representative of our school." The faculty agreed that he should try.

Tossing a few things into a bag, Jean-Jacques climbed aboard the coach for Paris. Representing his university, he felt, gave him every reason to expect to secure a place. Who could afford to miss such a golden opportunity to set foot in the land of the pharaohs and study their relics first hand? And wouldn't Cadet be overjoyed when he heard that his brother was going with Napoleon's expedition!

In Paris, the ministers and the generals, everybody and anybody who might have some influence, were beseiged by scholars and scientists, each urging that he be included. Jean-Jacques joined them. He sought the help of his friend and teacher, Monsieur de Sacy. "But I represent the University of Grenoble," he beseeched official after official. "I am a full professor of Greek! My knowledge will be of great value to General Napoleon!"

Details of his petition were taken down again and again,

with the calm assurance that the information would be placed before Napoleon.

Jean-Jacques Champollion enlisted the help of everyone he knew in Paris. For a while he thought he had been accepted, then he learned with dismay that the scholars who were going had already left Paris for Toulon. With a heavy heart, bitterly disappointed, he returned to Grenoble.

He consoled himself as best he could, reflecting that the others would bring back many treasures of the pharaohs to France, and if Napoleon should stay in Egypt, he might get another chance later.

Jean-François not only shared his brother's disappointment, but was even more disappointed that his brother had not been included in the expedition. "Never mind, Cadet," Jean-Jacques wrote, "I promise you that when the antiquities which they are bound to collect are in France, together we shall go to Paris and see them."

From the time of the Renaissance, scholars had struggled with the riddle of Egypt. That a great civilization had once flourished along the banks of the Nile was well known. Details of it, and the life of its people were, however, scarce and uncertain. What was known was based largely on speculation. Scholars *had* to depend upon Greek and Roman accounts to pursue their own studies, plus the few comments that could be found in the Old Testament. Ancient historians often misspelled Egyptian names, or sometimes changed them altogether, which deepened the mystery of the hieroglyphs.

Athanasius Kircher (1602-1680) was one of the first

"modern" scholars who made an attempt to decipher hiero-glyphics. Many others followed his trail. Kircher was a Jesuit who taught philosophy and mathematics at Würz-burg, Germany. Later he taught at Avignon, then Rome in mathematics, physics and Oriental languages. He resigned from the Collegio Romano so that he could devote the rest of his life to archaeological research, especially the study of hieroglyphics. Even in the seventeenth century there were those who considered Coptic, which was then still being spoken in Egypt, a form of the language of ancient Egypt.

The origins of the Copts are obscure. Under the Roman Empire, Egypt was peopled by mixed races. Some believe the Copts to be the descendants of the ancient Egyptians. The name Copt came into use after the Mohammedan con-quest of Egypt about A.D. 580. The word itself is derived either from Aegyptos (Egypt) or possibly from the town of Koptos. The Copts are one of the oldest Christian sects in the world and still practice their religion in its original form. The Copts hold a Monophysite doctrine which main-tains that the divine and human natures of Christ are one. Their church is headed by the Patriarch of Alexandria.

But inquiry into the origin of the Coptic language had not been pursued and, even if it did prove true that it was the spoken language of ancient Egypt, that still did not ex-plain the strange picture symbols. In Kircher's time it was too hazardous, except for the boldest of men, to penetrate the mysterious Middle East. It was Jean-François who was to prove Kircher mistaken in his views. Since he was a pioneer, Kircher's works have an interest, but he blazed a false trail which led many others astray in their efforts to solve the puzzle.

Nevertheless, Kircher's place is assured and he deserves credit. His contribution was mainly the bringing together, in a book, of a great collection of passages by Greek and Latin writers concerning Egypt. Further, he drew attention to the Coptic language through the large collection of manuscripts in the Vatican library written in that tongue.

All his young life Jean-François had heard political talk and was quite capable of taking part in such discussions. His contributions were mostly in the form of inquiry, but the questions he asked were usually so perceptive that he was given serious answers. Regardless of his scholarliness, the boy was not without boyish interests. He loved dogs and, at the moment, was collecting stories and listing the exploits of famous dogs.

"And what is all this about?" Jean-Jacques asked when he discovered his young brother's unusual hobby.

"Ah ha." Jean-François laughed gleefully. "I shall not tell you now, but later you will see! Do you know any stories of dogs that have had unusual adventures, Jacques?" he asked.

"Not any that I can think of right now," Jean-Jacques replied. "However, if you would like me to, I will try to find out if there are any such tales in Grenoble. And does this mean you are beginning to forget all about Egypt?"

Jean-François pulled a face. "Oh, you know better than that," he insisted.

"Well, I am glad," Jean-Jacques said, "but I was only teasing. You know, Cadet, I wonder if the hieroglyphs really can be read. Most of the people I've talked with still say they can be understood only as religious symbols. They do not accept the possibility that the signs may be a language. What a pity it is that there are not more examples available for comparison!"

In this manner Jean-Jacques did all that he could to fill the gaps in knowledge his brother longed to close. The boy seemed to fill his heart and soul with visions of the ancient pharaohs. Jean-François lived in a fever of excitement that bordered upon impatience.

"Let me see what progress you have been making with Greek and Latin," Jean-Jacques said.

Jean-François reached for a sheaf of papers and brought out a pile of books and clipped articles. "The exercises we get at school are not very difficult for me," Jean-François said. "I get through them very quickly. What I have been doing is to translate articles from French, the ones which seem difficult, into Greek and Latin. It is good practice for me."

Jean-Jacques looked through the translation and made a few corrections. "This is excellent," he said. "Of course you realize now, Cadet, that if you want to make the study of Egypt your life's work, you must master Greek. I don't think this will be hard for you. And, you know, once you have mastered one or two languages, others will come much more easily. All languages have certain things in common. If you have a good background in languages it will open many doors in the academic world." He laughed. "You won't become wealthy I fear, but it is an excellent way for a man to live his life. Let me warn you, Cadet, not to study too hard, because sometimes I worry that you will make yourself ill. Try to stay calm, and you must be patient. Most boys of your age think only of playing after school. You are very different and I understand that. But you must take care of yourself. It cannot be too long now before Papa will allow you to come to school at Grenoble. It may well be much sooner than you think."

"What do you mean by that?" Jean-François asked.

His brother tweaked his ear and laughed. "Never mind. You have your dog secrets, and I have mine! Something important may happen to me soon!" The boy pestered to know more but Jean-Jacques refused to clarify the mystery.

Napoleon's expedition to Egypt was ready to sail from Toulon on May 19, 1798. It was bigger by far than Napoleon had estimated and contained elements that seemed to prove he intended to stay a long time in Egypt. There were four hundred transports, escorted by warships, and there were more than 38,000 troops. More than one hundred scientists and experts of all sorts accompanied the expedition, some of them the finest minds of France. There had been many an intrigue among them to get included in Napoleon's voyage. The generals were jealous at the inclusion of the scholars. An elaborate study of Egyptian history, customs and art was planned, but the soldiers had no interest in the pharaohs and were bored by the long discussions. Occasionally one would fall asleep, to be rudely awakened and reprimanded by Napoleon.

The whole expedition was a fantastic conglomeration. Evidently a permanent French colony was to be set up in

Egypt. The enormous array of equipment the scholars carried with them made it apparent that they planned to set up schools. They carried hospital equipment, printing materials and a press, for they intended to start institutions of many kinds modeled after those of France. Obviously the French didn't intend merely to explore and return quickly to France with the knowledge gained from a single expedition. Perhaps the most important clue to Napoleon's plan was the presence of a group of clerks. These were to form the nucleus of a group around which he would build a civil service to administer Egypt.

Napoleon was lucky. Admiral Nelson's ships were off Toulon two days before the expedition sailed. There is no doubt about the fate of the expedition if the English admiral had caught the French ships. But Nelson was battered by a heavy storm. Some of his ships were badly damaged, so the admiral put in to the Mediterranean island of Sardinia for repairs. A swift passage was guaranteed the French fleet by strong winds and good weather, and by June 12 Napoleon had captured Malta.

From the moment he set foot ashore at Malta, Napoleon began to act like an emperor. He issued orders and decrees in his own name, not in the name of the French government. The once mighty Knights of the Order of Saint John, who had long ruled the island, had grown weak and corrupt. Napoleon, in the busy week he spent on Malta, seized their property and pensioned off the leading knights. He gave all the people French citizenship, then seized the property of their churches. The Maltese people did not resist, for they had no love for their own rulers. Napoleon sent about a hundred of the brightest Maltese youths to France to be educated, and he reorganized the university. He left a military governor in command of three thousand troops, then sailed for Alexandria on the Mediterranean coast of Egypt.

Nelson, hearing of the capture of Malta, guessed Napoleon must be making way for Alexandria. Nelson reached the seaport two days before the French fleet arrived. Not finding any trace of the French ships, he left for Sicily to replenish his supplies and learn the whereabouts of the French ships.

On July 2, less than a month after his victory at Malta, Napoleon had captured Alexandria and disembarked his troops and all their vital equipment. He soon learned that the English admiral had been at Alexandria.

In Egypt, Napoleon continued to act like an independent ruler. He issued proclamations, declared himself a defender of the Moslem faith and described himself as an ally of the sultan. He warned his soldiers under threat of severe punishment that they were to treat the local citizens with restraint and respect. For a time these actions kept the Beduin and other Moslem zealots pacified.

All this was rapidly accomplished and still there was no sign of Nelson. Napoleon left General Kleber in charge at Alexandria, with a force of six thousand men, and then, immediately taking the rest of his troops, he set out for Cairo. It was Napoleon's belief that the best strategy was to conquer and hold the capitol of Egypt. Other places could be taken later and subdued if they resisted. With control of Cairo, he could operate from a secure base.

Ahead lay nearly three awful weeks of marching across the scorching desert. Much of Napoleon's route now is heavy with lush green growth, for with the emergence of Egypt into the modern world, sweet water canals were built and the basically rich earth, drenched with precious water, quickly burst forth with life-sustaining crops. But at the time of Napoleon's march his troops lived off what the country and peasants could provide. Hostile Beduin, always keeping just out of sight, killed off any stragglers.

In preparing for the conquest of Egypt, by which he also hoped to make the Mediterranean a French lake, Napoleon had not taken into consideration the climate and character of the country. His troops were clad in heavy uniforms suitable only for colder climates. On the march to Cairo heat, hunger and thirst were their companions. The blazing sun beating at the sand created a dreadful glare which gave many of the troops serious eye trouble. Many straggled and died of thirst; many more, unable to cope with conditions, took their own lives. When the pyramids of Cairo came into sight Napoleon spurred his men on, crying, "Soldiers, from the summit of these pyramids forty centuries look down upon you!" Napoleon defeated an army of 18,000 cavalry and infantry just outside the capital. The Battle of the Pyramids, July 21, 1798, gave Napoleon control of Cairo. On July 24, he entered the city a conqueror.

Meanwhile, Nelson sailed into the Bay of Abukir, close by Alexandria, and destroyed or captured Napoleon's ships. Only two battleships and a frigate escaped the brilliant English admiral.

News of this rout reached Napoleon in Cairo by the

middle of August. Hiding his own disquiet, he calmed his officers, who became anxious at thus being cut off from France. Napoleon believed that action was the best antidote for lagging morale. Flies and desert pests of many kinds, the awful heat and cold nights tormented his troops unmercifully. Napoleon knew he had to move quickly.

Nelson provided Napoleon with his first taste of the strength of British sea power. With superb courage and calm determination, Napoleon faced up to the situation of finding himself marooned in Egypt. Addressing his men, he said, "Well! We must remain in this land, and come forth great, as did the ancients. This is the hour when characters of a superior order should show themselves." With a glitter in his eye he added, "The English will, perhaps, compel us to do greater things than we intended."

As a first step to lulling the fears of the population, Napoleon set up a government in Cairo that included nine prominent Egyptians. This was a wise move which temporarily allayed fears, but never since the days of the Roman conquest had so many Europeans been seen in Egypt at one time. The French seemed to be everywhere and resentment smoldered. Napoleon succeeded in getting the leaders of the Moslem religious centers of Cairo, Mecca and Tripoli to declare the French "friends of Islam," which also helped still any threat of panic. But this did not long hold in check the fanatical passions of the Arabs.

News of the defeat at Abukir reached the Turks. Constantinople declared war on France, and the news caused a great uprising in Cairo. The natives were put down, but several hundred French soldiers died in the effort.

While this was happening, Napoleon's scientists and experts had not been idle.

As soon as he had secured Cairo, in August, Napoleon founded the Institute of Egypt and put Monsieur Monge, one of his experts, at the head of it. His men erected their own buildings and took over others, which they made into libraries and laboratories. Much of the scholars' equipment had been lost with the sunken fleet, but the French experts improvised workshops to make what they needed and soon had serviceable instruments at their disposal. Also, something hitherto unknown in Egypt, Napoleon established a printing press and published a newspaper, *Courier de l'Egypte*. A geographic survey of the country was begun, keeping the map makers and artists busy. First a military hospital was set up, then a civilian hospital.

The architects, artists and other experts had been sent off to study the relics of the pharaohs. They came back to Cairo from Thebes, Luxor, Karnak and other ancient centers of Egyptian rule laden with sketches, statuary, copies of inscriptions and all sorts of antiquities. Many copies of hieroglyphic inscriptions were made. Their work was the basis of the monumental *Description of Egypt*.

From this beginning eventually grew the new science of Egyptology. Some of the material these men collected found its way back to France.

One great temple complex in excellent preservation was discovered at Dendera, on the left bank of the Nile. The site of this temple was correctly placed, later, in what became known as Upper Egypt. To reach it, the members of the expedition had sailed far up the Nile, almost to Thebes.

This great structure was to be the cause of dissension and controversy among scholars in Europe for many years when sketches of it and its inscriptions reached Paris and were published.

Napoleon had courage. With retreat to Europe cut off by Nelson, he crossed the forbidding Sinai Desert with 13,000 men. The Suez Canal had not yet been built. In Syria he destroyed Turkish troops who were assembling to fight against him, but Acre proved invincible and Napoleon had to retreat. Until this time Napoleon had not been a brutal man, but he now ordered three thousand prisoners massacred. He could not be burdened with caring for them on the return across the blistering Sinai Desert. In twenty-six days he reached Cairo to continue his consolidation of the city. News reached him in Cairo that a force of 18,000 men, Turkish troops, had landed at Abukir. Napoleon set out after them and cut them to pieces.

At Abukir, Napoleon learned that the political scene in France was more confused than ever. Leaving General Kleber in charge in Egypt, on August 21, 1799, he secretly sailed for France in a frigate that had survived Nelson's attack.

The return voyage to France was a hazardous one. Sometimes, when the wind changed course, the small vessel bearing Napoleon would be blown back over the painfully covered miles made that day. A constant watch had to be kept for British warships. Hugging close to the coast of Africa, the vessel slowly reached the narrows that separate Africa and Europe. After a three-week voyage, Napoleon

found the narrow straits guarded by a British warship. Under cover of night, with all lights out, Napoleon's ship slipped past the British. They reached the safety of Corsica, where lack of wind kept them becalmed for several days. There was much rejoicing in Corsica, for the people revelled in the glory surrounding Napoleon. This was the last time Napoleon saw his homeland. Leaving Corsica, Napoleon's ship was seen by a British ship that chased Napoleon almost to the coast of France. Hastening on to Paris, Napoleon was greeted with wild ovations wherever he stopped along the way.

The Directory had lasted four years. These years had been marked by corruption and incompetence that left the Directory teetering and ready to be tumbled. There was constant friction between the directors and the members of the legislature. Unscrupulous individuals schemed to fill their own pockets regardless of the welfare of the nation.

Napoleon had left France a strong nation. He returned to find that, in addition to domestic incompetence, the aggressiveness of the directors in foreign policy had forced England, Russia and Austria to form a new coalition against France. This coalition had succeeded in driving the French out of Germany and Italy and an invasion of France itself looked highly probable.

Napoleon allied himself with a group of politicians who, for various reasons, wanted to change the French constitution. With the leader of this group, the Abbé Sieyès, Napoleon plotted the *coup d'état* that was to bring the downfall of the government. The directors were to be forced to resign. Faced with the loss of its executive, the legislature would appoint a committee to revise the constitution. Naturally enough, Napoleon and Sieyès would be members of that committee. Though Napoleon was quite willing to use him, he despised Sieyès, referring to him as "that cunning priest." The *coup d'état* of November 9 and 10, 1799, was successful and the road to Empire lay open before Napoleon.

When the councils of the Ancients and the Five Hundred met, they abolished the Directory. In its place they appointed Napoleon, Sieyès and Duclos as First Consuls of France and then retired for four months. Barras lost his position in this struggle for power. Bowing to the determination of his former protégé, he quietly retired to his home in the country to write his memoirs.

Optimism ran high in France. Investment in government bonds doubled in just a week. Napoleon had been named first of the three consuls and the *coup d'état* was hailed by the people, who rejoiced at the prospect of peace. Rapidly, Napoleon restored order in France. England spurned his offers of peace, but by separate treaties and more military victories Napoleon managed to restore peace in Europe for a time. For this, a grateful French nation named him First Consul for life.

Napoleon's expedition into Egypt set the academic world afire. Scholars brought back with them artifacts of the pharaohs, drawings of fantastic animals, temples and pyramids and other wonders of the ancient world that were scattered all over the deserts of Egypt. The material, organized and published in the *Description of Egypt*, would be the foundation for the new science of Egyptology, but so far, all this wealth from an ancient civilization had no meaning.

Thus did Napoleon's conquests carry Jean-François Champollion a little further toward the fame predicted by the magician Jacquou.

CHAPTER **5**

OFF TO GRENOBLE

In 1799, when Jean-François was nine years old, one of those remarkable coincidences occurred which seemed to accent his life's purpose. A copy of the newspaper Napoleon had founded, the *Courier de l'Egypte*, turned up in the bookshop at Figeac. Jean-François pounced on it as if it were the greatest treasure in the world. At that moment, for him and posterity, it was!

"Papa, listen!" he said, almost getting his words mixed up in his eagerness to speak. "Listen to this article!" He read it to his father.

"Well, what is all the excitement about?" his father wanted to know.

"But don't you see, Papa, the slab of stone they have found in Egypt has writing on it! There are three languages, and one is Greek!"

"You just read that much to me, François," his father remarked.

"But, Papa, Jacques reads and speaks Greek! This stone may mean that we can learn to read hieroglyphics. Oh, Papa, I wish Jacques were home now."

The article was a report on the discovery of the Rosetta Stone in Egypt. This stone is a slab of polished black basalt, three feet nine inches long, two feet four inches wide, and eleven inches thick. French soldiers discovered it while they were repairing the ruins of Fort Rashid, close to the town of Rosetta, in the Nile delta.

There was some controversy surrounding the identity of the finder of this slab of black basalt in 1799. Whoever found it, it is one of the most important discoveries ever made in Egypt.

The remarkable thing about this slab of black basalt was that it bore inscriptions in three languages: hieroglyphics, demotic, and Greek. Demotic comes from the Greek and means belonging to, or of the people; in this case, the term applied to the simplified script used by the common people. Many scholars jumped to the conclusion that the Greek would provide an easy key that would make possible the interpretation of the hieroglyphic and demotic texts on the stone slab.

They soon found that they could read and understand the Greek inscription, but the demotic puzzled them and they found no clue to decipher the hieroglyphics.

Jean-Jacques had a surprise for his family on his next visit to Figeac. At the first evening meal after he arrived, with Jean-François looking on, he announced his news. First, he explained to them that he hoped soon to obtain an increase in his salary. Then he described to them dark-haired, petite Zoë Berriat. He told them how much he had fallen in love with her and that as soon as he received his increase in pay, they intended to marry. "We are," he said, "engaged now, and Zoë's family approves."

He talked of Pauline, Zoë's sister, and her parents. "They are a good family," he said, "and I know you will like Zoë. She is so clever, and well educated, and she has a delightful sense of humor." He smiled awkwardly. "I feel miserable when I'm away from her."

Monsieur and Madame Champollion had no objection to their elder son's engagement. He was still young, it was true, but as his father pointed out, "You have been a good son to us. You seem to be making excellent progress in Grenoble and I am sure you will not do anything foolish."

"A man should have a wife," Madame Champollion said, "and I am glad you feel that soon you will be able to support one. If this Zoë is as you describe, then I am sure you will be well taken care of when you are married."

Jean-François whooped. "Ha, ha!" he cried, "That's the secret you wouldn't tell me last time you were home, isn't it?"

Jean-Jacques grinned back at his brother. "Yes," he said, "yes, it is."

"Will you bring Zoë to Figeac next time you come?" Jean-François asked eagerly.

Jean-Jacques laughed, happy that his family approved of his plans and shared his hopes. "As to that, Cadet, I cannot say now. We shall see. Marriage is an expensive business, you know."

In 1801, Sir Ralph Abercromby landed with British troops at Abukir. After the fierce Battle of Alexandria, in

which Abercromby lost his life, the French were routed.
The British were determined to contain Napoleon, who was
becoming far too powerful to suit them. General Hutchin-
son took command and instantly marched on Cairo. There
the French were again defeated. By the first of September,
the French troops in Egypt sailed for France, and the British
captured the enormous quantity of antiquities gathered by
the French. Many treasures destined for the Louvre went
instead to the British Museum. Among them was the Rosetta
Stone, which is still displayed there.

Happily for French scholars, one of Napoleon's generals
had the hobby of studying Hellenism. He undertook to
translate the Greek inscription from the Rosetta Stone.
French scholars, at least, had that much to study. Later,
plaster casts were made from the stone in London and sent
to Paris. The message, as translated from the Greek, was a
decree of the Egyptian priesthood.

In 1801, the same year as Napoleon's defeat in Egypt,
after long consideration that finally led to a decision, Jean-
Jacques returned to Figeac. The government in Paris had
a growing awareness of France's need for capable men of
all kinds and a system was introduced whereby brilliant
students could receive government aid. This knowledge
played its part in Jean-Jacques's decision to press his father
over Jean-François's education. Though he was fully aware
of his own considerable talents as a linguist, Jean-Jacques
was certain that his eleven-year-old brother would become
a far more brilliant scholar. He had had long talks with their
father and eventually succeeded in convincing him that it

was neither right nor fair to Jean-François to keep the boy in Figeac any longer.

"For myself, I intend to teach," Jean-Jacques declared. "If any great honor or fame comes to this family it will be from Cadet. With his schooling and my personal tutoring I am sure he can easily pass the tests and become a government student, so there will be no need for you to worry about school fees. Also, Zoë and I will be married as soon as I return to Grenoble. She knows all about Cadet and you can be sure she will take good care of him." And so it was agreed.

Shortly after Jean-Jacques and Zoë Berriat married, Jean-François went to Grenoble. He had no difficulty with his exams and was accepted as a government-sponsored pupil, just as his brother had predicted. With the extra tutoring his brother gave him, he began to make rapid progress. Jean-François was enthralled by the beauty of the countryside about Grenoble, and he was keenly interested in every detail, for this was the land of his father's origin.

Not many cities in France have a finer situation or so beautiful a setting. Grenoble stands on the left bank of the Isère River, in a lovely, fertile valley. Hills and mountains sweep up steeply from the right bank of the river, crowned by a *bastille* (fortified castle) north of the city. To the east are the Savoy Alps (Haute-Savoie) dominated by the summit of Mont Blanc. Westward are the mountains of Saint Nizier. There are many open spaces in the town offering fine views, but in the tortuous streets every view seems blocked by hills and mountains.

In addition to being a university city, Grenoble was the

71

seat of a bishop. Grenoble had a population of about 25,000 people. The city had, originally, been fortified by the Roman Emperor Diocletian (A.D. 245-313). As in many old cities, the streets were capricious, twisting and winding in every direction. Some of them dated from the days of Diocletian; others were medieval. They were lined with old houses that created an atmosphere of peace and charm.

In earlier days, Grenoble had been the chief city of the province of Dauphiné. Grenoble's prosperity and importance rested on liqueurs, leather, straw hats, paper, cement and lime products. Today, Grenoble is the capital city of the Department of Isère.

The Dauphinois are a devout, independent people with strong democratic feelings. More than once there had been trouble with the government in Paris because of the independence of the provincial government. Their intellectual self-pride could certainly be justified. At the end of the eighteenth century the city could boast of many learned societies, some of them as fine as any to be found in Paris. In Figeac, Jean-François had been surrounded by an intellectual atmosphere since his earliest memories, but it was nothing compared with the world of fine minds, wit and culture he entered into in Grenoble.

Marriage suited Jean-Jacques and he was very happy with Zoë. Zoë had long realized that there was an unusual closeness between her husband and his young brother. She was a very intelligent woman and helpful to her husband in his work as well as being a capable housekeeper. Their house in Grenoble, though not large, was attractive and comfortable. The front door could be reached from left or right by a series of curved steps that rose a few feet from the ground to the door sill. Trim lawns surrounded the house and a small fountain played into a pond, which contained aquatic plants.

Zoë had worried at first about the attachment of her husband to his brother, and it was with some relief that she finally met Jean-François. She took an instant liking to the dark-skinned, handsome boy.

"So you are Cadet," she said. "Jacques has told me much of you. Sometimes"—she chuckled merrily—"he talks of nothing else. He has high hopes for you, Cadet." Bubbling with enthusiasm, she said, "Since you are so fond of Egypt, and could almost pass for an Arab I am sure, I think we should change your name!" She put a finger to her chin, eyes twinkling, as she regarded Jean-François, considering the matter. "Yes," she said finally, "I have it! I think we shall call you Sagîr!"

"Sagîr?" Jean-François said. "What does that mean?"

"In Arabic the name is the equivalent of Cadet."

"Oh, I like that very much," Jean-François exclaimed, and within the family the name stuck for the rest of his life.

"Do you know Arabic?" Jean-François asked Zoë, with some awe.

"I know something of several languages," Zoë said smiling. "How do you think I succeeded in marrying your brother?"

"Now I shall have to learn Arabic, too," Jean-François said, "so that we can speak it together."

The first few days in Grenoble, Jean-François wandered the city and explored its many side streets. He delighted in the deep gorges slashed with great outcroppings of rock through which the river flowed, and admired the fine bridges that crossed it.

"Well, Sagîr," said his brother after one of the lad's wanderings, "how do you like our Grenoble?"

"It's very fine," Jean-François replied. "What a wonderful library you have at the lyceum. *There* is where I expect to spend a lot of time! I've never seen so many books gathered in one place! But I've been everywhere. Today, Jacques, I climbed all the way up to the *bastille* on the other side of the river!"

"Then it's no wonder you look tired." His brother smiled.

Jean-François liked the Berriat family and, from the first meeting, the strong romantic streak in his nature drew him instantly to Zoë's sister Pauline, even though she was six years older than he was. For a good while everything went smoothly. Jean-François said to his brother, "I feel as if I have always known Zoë and her family."

Very soon Jean-François knew Grenoble physically and could relate its history. The speed with which Jean-François mastered facts and made them his own never ceased to amaze his brother. The boy never seemed to forget anything. There were other things, too, that Jean-François would have to learn. Deep in his love of history, the youth had not, so far, shown much interest in current events, except in general terms. Nevertheless, he needed to be appraised of facts, for the times were still extremely troublesome and there were sharp divisions of loyalty in Grenoble.

"The Dauphinois," Jean-Jacques explained, "are mostly in favor of a republican form of government. I am myself,

74

which is one reason this city appeals to me. There is an enlightenment here and a strong love of liberty. We have our rogues and scoundrels, too." He laughed. "And sometimes they are encountered in the most unlikely places!" He told his young brother that he was wise to concentrate on his studies and not to become too opinionated, stressing the need for caution in stating his views.

The seriousness of his brother's attitude caused Jean-François to think. It was as if he wanted once and for all to settle in his mind just what he believed himself. After thinking the matter over he wrote an essay, more or less a message to himself. In this essay he set down his views that a republican form of government was the only one under which men could live in freedom and liberty, able to pursue truth wherever it might lead. From this view he never swerved.

"Tell me," Jean-François asked one day, "have any antiquities from Egypt reached Grenoble yet?"

"I have not forgotten," his brother replied. "There is a man here who went with the expedition to Egypt. He is away now, but when he returns, the very first opportunity, I shall arrange for you to meet him."

The news thrilled Jean-François.

At Grenoble, working with a heavy schedule of study, a deeper bond of warmth and comradeship enfolded the brothers. Jean-Jacques devoted much of his time to the tutoring of Jean-François, and soon the lad began to prove the profit he made from this extra tutoring. Zoë fully approved this, so there was no friction in the house. Jean-François developed far beyond the average student who attended classes with him at the lyceum. This caused some jealousy of which, at first, Jean-François was not aware.

Jean-François astonished his brother again with the speed of his mastery of Greek and Latin. Having accomplished this, the boy immediately began to study Hebrew, making equally fast progress.

The admiration and affection Jean-Jacques felt toward his young brother moved him to a very noble and, indeed, unusual action. Because of the similarity of their names, he feared other people would confuse them and he did not want to take any credit away from what his brother might accomplish. Jean-Jacques, with Zoë's full approval, began to call himself Champollion-Figeac. Later, he dropped Champollion altogether, calling himself simply Figeac. When Jean-François discovered this, he repaid the compliment by addressing himself as Champollion le Jeune (the younger). This changing of names later caused scholars some trouble. Sometimes Jean-Jacques has even been confused with his father.

There were times when Jean-Jacques grew anxious about his young brother. The boy was so sure of himself that some people began to consider him opinionated and tactless —failing to see that it was eagerness for truth that sometimes made his manner abrupt. Though sensitive to criticism, Jean-François made no effort to hide his impatience with people he believed to be wrong in their views. He burned energy at a furious rate, as though he feared the passage of time in his frantic pursuit of knowledge. Sometimes he felt a little out of sorts, but, for the most part, he ate well and slept soundly, seeming none the worse for the long hours he spent poring over his beloved books.

In Grenoble, Jean-François developed his intellectual powers rapidly. He was not one of the rowdy students at the lyceum, nor could he be described as antisocial. In fact, when the legions of Napoleon swept toward Grenoble, Jean-François seized a tricolor banner. Waving it over his head he raced toward the tower of the lyceum. After a laborious climb to the top of the tower, he tore down the hated lily banner of the Bourbons and ran up the tricolor of the Republic.

Jean-Baptiste Joseph Fourier was himself only thirty-three years old when Jean-François was introduced to him by Jean-Jacques. But Fourier was already very famous and had experienced some amazing adventures as one of the scholars who accompanied Napoleon to Egypt. During the time he spent there, Fourier served Napoleon well. In addition to his scientific studies, Fourier was given very important political duties, which he carried out with distinction. He was appointed Secretary to the Institute of Cairo, a creation of Napoleon's, and in this post he was more or less responsible for governing about half of Egypt.

When he returned to France, Fourier had been made Prefect of Grenoble. There, the finest minds in the city gathered about him and formed a scholarly elite. Fourier specialized in mathematics and physics. His most renowned work, *The Analytical Theory of Heat*, made history in the spheres of mathematical and physical science.

Fourier was incredulous when he first met the young Champollion. To Fourier, who knew them well, Jean-François looked more like an Egyptian than the Egyptians! Fourier said as much, and for the rest of his life Jean-François was frequently referred to as "the Egyptian." Fourier was deeply impressed by the youth's knowledge of languages, his high intelligence and eagerness to learn. This young man, he felt sure, was destined to do something extraordinary with his life.

The next meeting of Fourier and Jean-François came when Fourier made a tour of inspection of Grenoble's schools, a part of Fourier's duties as prefect. Fourier engaged in a debate with Jean-François, and he was astounded at the youth's skill. Wanting to know this exceptional student still better, Fourier invited him to his home.

"My brother told me you brought back some relics from Egypt," Jean-François said. "May I please see them, Monsieur Fourier?"

"Of course, François, of course you may." Fourier showed him some fragments of papyri covered with hieroglyphs and some stone tablets bearing more of the strange signs.

"Has anybody read the hieroglyphs yet?" Jean-François asked.

"No," replied Fourier. "There are a lot of 'explanations' being offered, some of them by men who ought to know better. Some of the ideas I have heard are so foolish they border on the ridiculous! There are those who are giving them serious attention, however. It may be of some help to them when we publish the report of our findings in Egypt during the expedition. But nobody, to the best of my knowledge, has had any real success in deciphering any of the hieroglyphic symbols."

Jean-François fingered the tablets and papyri with a quiet concentration, almost as if he were trying to look *through* the opaque stone and parchment, forcing them to reveal the meaning of their symbols. Suddenly he turned to Fourier and, with a positiveness that startled the older scholar, said, *"One day I shall decipher them. I shall read these hieroglyphs!"*

Fourier studied the intenseness of eleven-year-old Jean-François's expression and choked back the "humorous comment to a child" he was about to utter.

This incident with Fourier Jean-François never forgot. At that moment, though he scarcely realized it, he had committed himself to a seemingly impossible task.

The brilliance of this young lad from Figeac was the talk of the salons in Grenoble. Some people were already calling him a linguistic genius. Jean-François knew his purpose now. Everything he studied pointed in one direction. If he were to succeed in deciphering the hieroglyphs, he must learn all he could about ancient Egypt and all the world's ancient writings and languages. He was impatient for the publication of the report of the expedition to Egypt. So sure was he of the path he had to take, it didn't even occur to him that someone else might decipher the hieroglyphs first.

In 1802, now twelve years old, Jean-François wrote his first book, *A History of Famous Dogs*. This, then, had been the purpose of his collecting dog stories. He grew irritated that it had taken him so long; but he had discovered that there were few well-planned reference books from which to work. Promptly he made up his own table, which he entitled "Chronology from Adam to Champollion"!

By the time he was thirteen, Jean-François was studying Arabic, Syrian, and had made a start on the very ancient Coptic tongue. He took up the study of old Chinese, for there was a theory subscribed to by some scholars that the ancient Egyptians may have come from China to settle beside the river Nile. All that Jean-François studied led inexorably to the Egypt of the pharaohs.

Though he had little interest in outdoor activities, other than walking, Jean-François looked healthy. He was not tall, but his firm, slender body seemed full of strength. Mostly it was the handsome dark head, the fine-boned face full of magnetism that caught people's attention. He carried himself well and people generally turned to look at him a second time when he passed on the streets. When he talked upon matters he loved, he seemed to vibrate with the intensity of his desire to be clearly understood. He seldom stumbled for a word, but he would repeat the most minute details in order that the truth, as he saw it, be conveyed. Slowly he was learning to control his excessive enthusiasms. It was not easy for him, but it was a blessing that his willfulness was directed into a constructive channel.

Through the intervention of Fourier, and with his assistance, materials otherwise unavailable in Grenoble were acquired for Jean-François to study. He studied ancient Persian, East Indian religious writings and other rare texts, and by the time he had reached the age of seventeen, Jean-

François had made his first table of Egyptian pharaohs and their succession.

To create his table of the pharaohs, Jean-François used the Old Testament as well as ancient works in Latin, Greek, Arabic and Coptic. Hebrew was also helpful to him in this task. It was a remarkable accomplishment, for so little was known about contemporary Egypt, let alone the Egypt of the pharaohs. Archaeology was hardly a science thus far, and no one had yet taken pick and shovel to dig in the desert sands in search of that ancient civilization. Jean-François was wrong in many instances, but it was better to have his table, mistakes and all, than to have no reference work. Some scholars were deeply impressed by this effort. Others, from varying motivations, dismissed the "Table of the Pharaohs" as fanciful and inaccurate.

Between 1809 and 1816 the long report of the expedition to Egypt was published. There was a wealth of firsthand information in this work.

La description de l'Egypte contained innumerable copies of hieroglyphic inscriptions. These had been copied from temples, steles and statuary. Within this work was collected, for the first time in one reference source, more observations on the ancient relics of Egypt than had ever appeared before.

Though far from a complete picture, it revealed for the first time a portion of the fantastic civilization that had once flourished along the river Nile. For all its value, this report was inadequate because hieroglyphics still awaited translation. The material made available to scholars through this work pushed the academic world of Europe into an almost frantic period of activity. The scholars were almost fighting among themselves to get their views heard and considered. Devotees of the science of Egyptology doubled and tripled in number.

CHAPTER **6**

THE STUDENT BECOMES
A TEACHER

The inscribing and placing of stone steles, or slabs, in temples was a common practice in ancient Egypt. Usually, these steles were made for the purpose of promulgating and perpetuating matters of national interest, such as laws, decrees, dedications and records of victories and other outstanding events, or the completion of buildings and similar undertakings. The practice lives on today in the dedication of bridges, dams and the laying of cornerstones in buildings by prominent people.

Great discoveries are almost always the product of many isolated events which happen along the way to knowledge. Small things an individual might discover, of no apparent importance in themselves, often provide vital links to carry a project forward. As early as 1797, when Jean-François first heard the magic name Egypt, a few trained scientists had made observations which flicked slightly the veil that shrouded the mystery of hieroglyphics. These men were serious scholars, but their comments were lost in the babble of "interpretations" that followed publication of Napoleon's expedition's *La description de l'Egypte.*

George Zoega, a Danish scholar of wide renown, had suggested that certain figures of animals, birds and plants used in hieroglyphics might represent sounds which could well be letters. And there were others, including Monsieur de Sacy, who were beginning to hope and to look for something other than symbolic religious meaning in the peculiar signs.

Belief was steadily spreading that hieroglyphics *was a written language,* applicable to the purposes of history and common life in ancient Egypt, as well as containing religious, even mythical, symbols. But the key to reading the language, if it was a language, had yet to be discovered, and insistence is not proof. This observation, too, was lost in the furor that followed publication of *La description de l'Egypte.*

Jean-François fixed these varying and isolated comments firmly in his mind.

In 1804, the Senate in Paris proclaimed Napoleon Emperor of France. He had brought peace to Europe by conquering large portions of it, and it appeared that an age of new glory was ahead. In some respects it was. When he ascended the throne, Napoleon made many changes in France. He established the University of France and linked administratively all public *lycées* to it. He restored to the nobility its lost privileges and restored the rights of the Church. Napoleon made war profitable by confiscating money, property, works of art and, in this fashion, at least stilled the drain on the French treasury. The needs of his large armies caused a rise in employment as workers turned out the uniforms and equipment he needed in his campaigns of conquest. For a while France, under the new regime, earned as much money as the country spent, and enjoyed the rare luxury of a balanced budget. The country took on a semblance of stability, but Frenchmen who preferred the republic did not like the turn of events.

The following year, 1805, war again broke out between France, Russia and Austria. Napoleon defeated the Austrians and Russians. He advanced through the German States, entered Vienna, and won a great victory at Austerlitz on December 2.

In 1806, the emperor was in Berlin. He destroyed what was left of the Holy Roman Empire, whose boundaries once included parts of Italy, Germany, Austria, Switzerland and the Tyrol as well as a large part of France and the Netherlands. In 1807 Napoleon, firmly established as the ruler of France, created the Confederation of the Rhine from what was once a group of German principalities, duchies and independent cities. Most were German, but the Confederation included within its boundaries parts of Austria, Prussia, Bohemia, Hanover and Bavaria.

The boundaries of Napoleon's empire now far exceeded those of the former kingdom of France. Despite the Senate's proclamation, Napoleon knew that in reality he was a usurper and the Bourbons might still regain their power. He was determined to establish a dynasty and make his reign legitimate in the eyes of the rest of the world. The French people had begun to believe that he was an invincible hero.

But through edict and decree, the hand of the despot gradually made itself known. Jean-François was enthusiastic about the emperor and the glittering new France he ruled. He believed that from Napoleon's leadership there would grow an enlightenment that would raise France above all nations in its artistic and cultural and scholarly accomplishments. Often under totalitarian rule, great incentive has been given to scholarship and artistic endeavor. Were not the Medici an outstanding example? Perhaps, when he was done fighting, Napoleon would follow their example. And who could deny the priceless results obtained by the expedition to Egypt, even though it ended as a disaster for France. Yet, as he witnessed Napoleon making princes and rulers of his brothers, marrying his sisters into the nobility, Jean-François doubted Napoleon would have much time for anything other than politics and more war.

In many ways, 1807 was a disturbing year for Jean-François, and the willfulness of his actions proved distressing to many others. Though he was only seventeen, he considered himself very much a man of the world. Seeing his brother's happiness in marriage, he determined to marry himself. He did not stop to think how he was going to support a wife. Nor were his actions those of a young man desperately in love; rather he made an intellectual decision that he wanted to be married and married he would be. In the romantic style of the day, young men considered love an enobling experience and spoke in such phrases as "deep devotion" even if the girl or lady in question was hopelessly beyond reach. Despairing love was a wonderful thing to suffer.

Jean-François was no different, in this respect, than other young men of his time. Brashly, he declared his love for Zoë's sister, Pauline Berriat, completely ignoring the fact that she was quite a few years older than himself. Unfortunately, Pauline, who was fond of him, permitted his attentions and allowed him to pay her court. She, too, gave no thought to how Jean-François was going to support her.

For once, Jean-Jacques was very angry with his brother and they quarreled. "How could you permit such a thing to occur, Sagîr?" he asked. "There is so much that you have to do and have yet to learn. You are far too young to 'pledge your honor' to Pauline. This attachment can only cause trouble and you should end it before it goes any further. Not the least concern is how you are going to earn a living."

Jean-François could be very stubborn. "Far from ending it," he said, "I intend to marry Pauline as soon as possible! I shall find work of some kind to support us."

The brothers discussed the situation to no avail. Jean-François seriously considered moving to Paris. There, he felt sure, he could find some sort of a post that would earn him enough money to send for Pauline and marry her.

Zoë was deeply distressed over her sister and Jean-François, yet she also realized there were no other prospects of marriage for Pauline. The rest of the family were outraged by the ridiculous liaison. Pauline's father was furious!

"How dare you declare your intentions to my daughter?" Monsieur Berriat raved at Jean-François. "What possible prospects have you for supporting her? I demand that you apologize to Pauline and I wish to hear no more of this absurd notion of marriage! What *can* you offer?" he demanded. "There you are, locked away at the lyceum every day studying old books and languages that are of absolutely no use to anyone! You are scarcely more than a boy and not fit for marriage!"

For once Jean-François was without self-confidence. He mumbled something about prestige and honors and his hopes of a teaching career.

"Prestige, honors! *You* can't eat those, Champollion. Neither can *my* daughter!"

Jean-François soon learned that he was no longer welcome at the Berriat home. He continued, secretly, to meet with Pauline and she agreed that they might find the answer to their problem if Jean-François found a position in Paris. From this first brush with the realities of everyday living, Jean-François was seldom to be free of financial troubles of one degree or another. There was truth in Monsieur Berriat's observation. Prestige and honors, particularly at that time, did not necessarily bring financial rewards. And to add to the dilemma, Jean-François had a poor sense of business.

Pressure eased for a while in the trouble over Pauline, but only through another grief. In the summer of 1807, news came to Grenoble that the beloved mother, Madame Champollion, had died at the age of sixty in Figeac.

The authorities at the lyceum in Grenoble learned that young Jean-François was troubled and restive. He began to feel that he had exhausted the possibilities at Grenoble. He was anxious to move on to Paris, to immerse himself in the archives and museums there, for Paris was a treasure-house compared to Grenoble, and he was anxious to start earning a living.

Jean-François had not as yet actually made any detailed or specific effort to decipher the hieroglyphs. He was restraining himself, almost as if he were afraid of failure. Yet everything he did spelled EGYPT and was in preparation for the moment he would believe himself sufficiently equipped to combat this enormous self-imposed task. Concern over Pauline, realization of how much he had taken for granted while living with Jean-Jacques, made him nervous and irritable and it was hard for him to concentrate on his studies.

After a conference of the faculty at Grenoble, it was decided that the youth be invited to submit a paper, the subject to be of his own choosing. Though some members made no effort to hide their hostility and jealousy, they lacked the courage to openly belittle the brilliant student. Among themselves they muttered about his being given too much freedom, being pushed ahead too fast, and since they knew about Pauline, it was a simple matter for them to suggest this was a mark of instability in him.

Jean-François's directness made it easy for those who disliked him to turn dislike into something stronger. Zoë and Pauline, through friends who were wives of some of the faculty members, often heard disparaging remarks about Jean-François. They warned him to soften his attitude toward other people. But in the strength and eagerness of his youth, he had no patience with ignorance and deplored the

89

sight of men of little ability in commanding positions. He brushed aside the warnings. What did he care about idle gossip? Soon he would be moving to Paris anyway and he would have no further concern with such small-minded people.

The faculty expected a paper from Jean-François that would be something out of the ordinary, but none of them expected what was in store for them.

On September 1, 1807, Jean-François read his "paper." It was the introduction for a book he proposed to write, *Egypt Under the Pharaohs!* The entire faculty gathered to hear Jean-François Champollion read.

The dark-skinned, slim youth stood erect before the gathered professors. He trembled slightly, with excitement, his slender frame agitated by the force of his emotion—he knew he *must* make his points to his teachers. What Jean-François proposed was nothing less than an encyclopedic study of ancient Egypt in all its aspects.

As he read, occasionally brushing a fine hand through his dark curly hair, young Champollion held the teachers enthralled. They knew he was brilliant, but they had heard nothing like this before! Even the scholars in Paris had not dared so much. The logic of Jean-François's researches into ancient Egyptian history astounded his audience and gave powerful backing to his theses. There were gasps of amazement as he spoke of the sources of his gathered material: a mention from an ancient Coptic script, something from a Hebrew or an Arabic source. The enormous listing of sources represented hours and hours of reading and note-

taking in obscure reference books that few of the teachers had even heard of, much less read. All these mentions of the ancient Egyptians, from many languages and many previously unknown sources, Jean-François proposed to bring together in one coherent work in modern French, painting a picture of the times of the ancient pharaohs.

Jean-François produced a map he had made of the Nile Delta area and demonstrated how he proposed to explain the successions of the pharaohs, the rise and fall of dynasties and the changes that had occurred in the ancient civilization.

As he talked, his oriental looks added a touch of unexpected glamor. This young man had never *been* to Egypt, and had only read books and papers written by others in order to learn about the country. Yet here he was, showing a map, describing ancient Egypt, explaining it as if he had actually lived there! It was an unbelievable performance! His knowledge was profound, as those teachers who respected him could clearly see. He had so immersed himself in the times of the ancient pharaohs that, standing at the end of the room, he created an intriguing illusion that he had just stepped out of ancient Egypt into the nineteenth century! His conviction and sincerity carried all before him. Most of the faculty thrilled to the ideas Jean-François presented to them—there could be no denying the dedicated labor that had gone into this outline for *L'Egypte sous les Pharaons*—still there were those cynical enough to think he would never write the book he proposed.

When he finished speaking there was a hush, quickly followed by a buzz of intense excitement. Right then, the president of the lyceum jumped to his feet and embraced Jean-François.

Bubbling with good spirits, Professor Renauldon said, "My dear Champollion, we have decided that we should like you to join us on the faculty immediately! We are proud of you, proud of your accomplishments. We know, too, that this is as nothing to what you will accomplish. It is our hope that when the world recognizes your genius, you will remember us, the *first* to recognize that genius."

In one moment, then, from being a student, Jean-François became a highly regarded teacher at his own school. He was then seventeen years of age.

The proposal for the book, *Egypt Under the Pharaohs*, was a daring one. It was true that Jean-François had checked every source he could find that mentioned ancient Egypt. Still, the hieroglyphs had not been deciphered and, if they were, they could well prove Jean-François's proposals idiotic. However, though it had not yet been published, he had already written a study which was an attempt to prove that the great figures in the Old Testament were real people, not characters drawn from the rich imagination of some ancient scribe. Now he had proposed to do the same thing for the Egyptian pharaohs, identifying them, dating them, and placing them in proper chronological order in the story of ancient Egypt.

Jean-François had only seen sketches made at the time of Napoleon's expedition and the few items Fourier had been able to make available for him. He had built his theories so thoroughly that he had not the slightest doubt of the accuracy of his deductions or his ability to substantiate them at the proper time. Through studying ancient Coptic, he became convinced that this language, or some version of it, had been spoken by the ancient Egyptians.

As he was leaving the lyceum after reading his paper, Jean-François fainted, quite overcome by his great concentration with the faculty and the knowledge that he had carried nearly all of them with him. Jean-Jacques and Zoë accompanied him to his room and made him rest.

Fussing to make him comfortable, Zoë, genuinely anxious, moved about Jean-François. Jean-Jacques brought him a mug of red wine diluted with a little water to help him relax where he was stretched out on a sofa.

With pride in his accomplishment, but lacking any trace of braggadocio, Jean-François exclaimed, "What a day! What a triumph!"

"Sagîr, calm yourself," Zoë said. "Why must you always be so intense about everything? If you do not learn to relax and take things a little more casually you will make yourself ill."

"What will your father have to say about Pauline and me now, when he hears about this?" Jean-François said.

Zoë showed her exasperation. "Sagîr, you know my father well enough. He is a practical businessman and what happened today will not make the slightest impression on him. You have angered him and he is not a very forgiving man. Besides, even though you join the faculty, your salary will not be more than you need to support just yourself!"

"Ha, but Zoë, don't you see, this carries me much closer to Paris and a higher position."

94

Pauline Berriat entered the room, relieved to find that there was nothing really wrong with Jean-François. The events of the day were talked over again with Pauline, then they all began talking about Paris and the future prospects for Jean-François.

"Eventually, the sooner the better, I must get to Paris," he said emphatically. "For me, everything lies there. If I can save enough from my salary at the lyceum to last for a while, I can surely find a position good enough for me to send for you, Pauline."

"If you fall ill you won't be going anywhere," Zoë snapped.

"You are still very young, Sagîr, your time will come I am sure," Jean-Jacques said. "When that time does come I can help you with some introductions to people who can advise and perhaps help you."

"Even Monsieur Fourier is in Paris now! All the important Egyptologists are there," the youth insisted. "I need to be there, to be present when they announce their progress, not have to wait to learn of it perhaps weeks later. If I were in Paris and could mingle with the men working there, I could save myself a lot of time by avoiding duplication of their efforts and profiting from their errors. Surely after the success today, I ought to be able to find a teaching position or research work for one of the museums?" Slowly, Jean-François let himself relax.

One thing that drew Jean-François like a powerful magnet to Paris were the copies of the inscriptions of the famous Rosetta Stone. For the task ahead, he possessed some outstanding qualities. He had courage and an inventive mind. He was creative, highly imaginative, but he also possessed a strong sense of reality, which kept his imagination within the bounds of reason. Perhaps most important of all, he knew he would have to demonstrate the accuracy of his findings, for he had learned that opinions are not proof.

Despite the proof the Rosetta Stone offered, too many men calling themselves Egyptologists continued to cling to the old notion that hieroglyphics were symbols that could never be read as a language. They made no effort to try to find an alphabet or grammatical construction. Jean-François, though still bedeviled by the idea that the hieroglyphs were religious symbols, knew they proclaimed the same message as the Greek—but in what manner? How to find letters and words in the odd marks carved into the stone? The story on the stone gave Jean-François the weird feeling that he had been there when it was commissioned, so clear was the scene.

In his mind, Jean-François pictured a colorful event, with all its solemnity and elegance, that took place at Memphis in 195 B.C. All the brillance of the nobles in their finest costumes and jewels, the stirring of the crowds of ordinary people outside, were real to him.

He saw King Ptolemy V, Epiphanes, seated on his splendid throne in formal attire, arms crossed, bearing the wands of his high position. As trumpets blared, a long procession of priests and their attendants slowly made its way toward the throne and took their positions for the ceremony.

Soldiers and some higher officials formed a crescent about the king on his throne. More soldiers lined the walls of the temple. The leader of the priests made his way to the center of the crescent about the king, where, facing the monarch, he made obeisance. Solemnly he read the proclamation which granted divine honors to Ptolemy, loudly announcing the king's many virtues and great deeds which justified his being made a god. Now the priest concluded the ceremony: ". . . and in order that it may be known why the Egyptians pay honor to the god, the priests have decreed that this decree shall be inscribed upon a stele of hard stone in the writing of the divine words, and in the writing of the books, and in the writing of the Greeks, and that a similar stele shall be set up in the temple of the first, second and third order, side by side with the statue of the god Ptolemy, the ever living."

In 1808, when the time finally came, Jean-Jacques accompanied Jean-François on his first visit to Paris. Hours on end, for three days, the brothers were jolted about as their coach covered the rough roads to the capital. At night they stopped at inns and taverns along the way. It was a tiresome journey, but Jean-François was intensely animated and kept up a barrage of conversation about the Rosetta Stone and the hieroglyphs. His dark eyes were brilliant as he said to Jean-Jacques, "I have it in my power! I know I shall succeed in deciphering the hieroglyphic symbols!" Pounding his fist on his knee, he repeated emphatically, "*I know I will!*"

CHAPTER 7

PARIS

To verify the sort of conjecture made by Zoega and others, and in order to build upon it, three things were vitally necessary to deciphering the hieroglyphs. If the hieroglyphs were phonetic, the words they expressed must have belonged to the language spoken in the days of the pharaohs. It was necessary, therefore, first to establish what this language had been, and if any trace of it remained. Second, a large number of copies of inscriptions would be needed for the purpose of broad comparison and checking of individual characters that appeared in hieroglyphics. The third requirement was an authentic translation of hieroglyphics into a language that was known, and which could be read by modern scholars. If such a translation was found, chances were that it would be in Greek. Little by little, these three needs were met.

In the first instance, Quatremere produced his work, *Sur la langue et litterature de l'Egypte* (On the Language and Literature of Egypt). With beautiful insight, Quatremere had seen that Coptic was to ancient Egyptian what modern Italian is to Latin. It was still a long way from reading hieroglyphics, but a clue had been planted for whoever was sharp enough to pick it up.

Etienne Marc Quatremere, a noted orientalist, was employed in the manuscript department of the Imperial Library in Paris in 1807. His book, which he published in 1808, established that the language of the ancient Egyptians was, indeed, a form of Coptic. The veil shrouding the mystery was lifted a little more.

Quatremere's contribution was a valuable foundation. But it brought no immediate results. It did not explain the hieroglyphs nor did it explain the demotic script inscribed on the Rosetta Stone. The demotic script was written in horizontal lines from right to left. There appeared to be no connection at all between this script and the hieroglyphic script.

The publication of the results of the findings of Napoleon's expedition helped fill the second need, and provided a large number of copies of inscriptions for comparison. In addition, the material the British made available after their first adventures in Egypt swelled the collection.

The miraculous discovery of the Rosetta Stone in 1799 filled the third and most vital need, with its message written in hieroglyphics, demotic and Greek.

Some of the hieroglyphs at the beginning of the hieroglyphic text were missing, for the corner of the stele was broken off. The Greek message, after translation, yielded in essence the following information:

> In the ninth year of the king, who hath risen in the place of his father, the Lord of the double crown of the South and the North, whose image is great, who

hath established Egypt and made it prosperous—who is like unto Ptah the Great, and like unto Ra, the living image of Amen, the son of the Sun, Ptolemy, the ever living, beloved of Ptah—a decree: The priests who declare oracles, and the servants of the gods and the priests who enter into the sanctuary to array the gods in their apparel, and the scribes of the holy books, and the other priests who had come from the temples of Egypt to Memphis, to the festival of the reception of the exalted rank by King Ptolemy, who have gathered themselves together at Memphis, spake, saying: "Inasmuch as it hath happened that King Ptolemy the son of King Ptolemy and the Queen Arsinoe hath conferred many benefits upon the temples of Egypt, and upon all those who were under his royal dominion—and inasmuch as his heart is benevolently disposed towards the gods, and he hath given much money and much corn to the temples of Egypt, and he hath expended large sums in order to establish the peace of Egypt; and of the taxes and the dues to the government which exists in Egypt, one part he hath diminished, and one part he hath entirely abolished; and he hath given up the debts which the inhabitants of Egypt, and those who were under his royal dominion, owed to the king, and which formed a very large amount of money; and he hath set free from prison those who had been condemned to be there under judgments which had been given a long time ago; and the revenues of the gods, and the money and the grain which the people were obliged to contribute to the temples, and also the share of the vineyards and orchards which belonged to the gods, he hath commanded to remain as they had been formerly:

and in the matter of the priests he hath ordered that men shall pay no higher tax to become priests than they did up to the first year of his father's reign—and he hath taken great care that every honor which it was customary to pay to the gods, and every ceremony which it was customary to perform for them, shall be carried out in the proper manner; and he hath administered justice to all people, even as does Thoth, the twice great—and he hath taken care to send troops, both cavalry and ships against those who came to fight against Egypt by sea and by land, and hath in consequence expended a very large amount of money and grain in order that the temples and the inhabitants of Egypt might remain in peace—and the gods permitted him to slay the enemy, the troops who had gathered themselves together—and he caused them to suffer death upon wood [i.e. he crucified them]—and he hath conferred many benefits upon Apis and Mnevis, and other sacred animals of Egypt, far more than any of his ancestors; and he hath spent in a lavish and splendid manner whatsoever sums were needed for burying them in a suitable manner—and he hath built new temples and shrines and altars for the gods. . . ." The priests of all the temples of Egypt have passed a decree to increase the ceremonial observances of honor which are paid in the temples to King Ptolemy, the ever living—and have decided to set up a statue of King Ptolemy, which shall be called "Ptolemy, the Savior of Egypt," side by side with a statue of the Lord of gods, in every temple, and in the most prominent place thereof, and the priests shall worship the statues in all the temples three times each day—and they shall cause a divine image of King Ptolemy to appear with the golden shrines which are in all temples, and they shall set upon the shrine ten royal double crowns of gold, and upon each of the double crowns there shall be placed a serpent—and the thirtieth day of the month of Mesore, the birthday of the king, and the seventeenth day of the month of Paape, the day of reception by him of his exalted rank, shall be kept as days of festival in every temple in Egypt, and every month, on those days, burnt offerings and libations shall be made—and festivals and processions shall be established in the temples and in all Egypt in honor of King Ptolemy—and the priests in all the temples of Egypt, in addition to the titles which they already hold, shall have the title "Priests of the God who maketh himself manifest, whose deeds are beautiful [Ptolemy]," and this title shall be endorsed on all deeds and documents which are laid up in the temples, and shall be engraved on the priests' rings; and in order that it may be known why the Egyptians pay honor to the God . . . [Ptolemy] the priests have decreed that this decree shall be inscribed upon a stele of hard stone in the writing of the divine words [hieroglyphics], and in the writing of the books [demotic], and in the writing of the Greeks, and that a similar stele shall be set up in the temples of the first, second and third order, side by side with the statue of the god Ptolemy, the ever living.

It had been no problem to translate the Greek inscription on the Rosetta Stone. After it was done, attention focused on the demotic script. Some scholars thought this would be comparatively easy, but it was not. Little more progress was made for several years.

Jean-François, keenly aware of what was going on, spent his time building a solid vocabulary of Coptic and studying other dead languages which he thought might prove useful. Meanwhile, more great stone monuments covered with inscriptions reached Europe. These obelisks were soon to be found in most of the capital cities.

Monsieur Sylvestre de Sacy made the next important contribution to the solution of the mystery of demotic writing. He used a plan that is often followed in deciphering secret writings. The first step was to ascertain the number of different signs or characters. (Our alphabet, for example, has twenty-six letters.) Next was the task of discovering the groups or combinations of characters that occurred most frequently. These had to be determined, and the characters explained, by words of the language they were supposed to be written in. Since there was no proof of any other, it was natural to presume that the unknown tongue spoken by the ancient Egyptians had to be Coptic. Quatremere had already shown that this was probably so.

Monsieur de Sacy saw that the only sure way to proceed was to take the proper names that occurred in the Greek script on the stone and try to find their equivalent in demotic. Monsieur de Sacy was successful and, in 1802, declared his discovery of the names Ptolemy, Berenice and Alexander in the demotic script. Contrary to what many people believed, the name of Cleopatra did not appear on the Rosetta Stone.

Jan David Akerblad, a brilliant Swedish diplomat, went even further than de Sacy. In a letter to de Sacy, Akerblad explained that the groups of characters that de Sacy had discovered were names and could be broken down into individual letters. Akerblad formed an alphabet for nearly all the demotic characters. But he did not suspect that, in addition to letters, the demotic script employed symbolic signs. Neither did he suspect that the hieroglyphics employed phonetic signs as well as symbols. The hieroglyphs remained a mystery. These were valuable additions to decipherment of the demotic script, but progress ceased for a time. About half a dozen signs in the demotic script completely mystified the scholars.

Jean-François ignored completely the many attractions of the great city of Paris. He continued to study Sanskrit and Persian sacred writings, and went on building his mastery of Arabic and Coptic. He did call upon Monsieur Fourier. Fourier complimented him on the paper he had read in Grenoble, and wished him luck with the proposed book. But for the most part, Jean-François lost himself in the dusty archives of Parisian libraries and museums. Like a man possessed, he dashed from one institute to another whenever he learned that such a place contained anything to do with ancient Egypt or the Coptic language. So absorbed was he in pursuit of mastering Coptic that he kept personal journals in that language and once observed to Jean-Jacques, "I speak Coptic to myself!" He also commented wryly, "Every day my Coptic dictionary is getting thicker. The author, meanwhile, is getting thinner!"

(Nearly half a century later one of the journals Jean-François kept in Coptic was the cause of a famous and amusing gaff. The journal fell into the hands of another French scholar. This unfortunate man mistook the entries for an authentic record dating from the time of Marcus Aurelius Antoninus and produced a very learned paper on Jean-François's journal!)

Before the great treasures of the Louvre, Jean-François was like a child, filled with wonderment. The magnificent group of buildings that comprise the Louvre stretch for almost a mile along the right bank of the river Seine. Many kings had a part in what has finally resulted in this beautiful structure. In the Middle Ages it was a strong castle. Under Charles V it became a mansion and by the time of Louis XIV it was an elegant château. The Louvre as an art museum began with Francis I (1494–1547). Leonardo da Vinci, dying and in the service of Francis I, finally let the king have the one painting he had always treasured himself, and would never sell, the *Mona Lisa*. The *Mona Lisa* still holds court in the great hall of the Louvre.

The long history of this site makes it an enduring memorial to French history. It bears testimony, too, to the creative ideas loosed by the French Revolution, for the present arrangement, opening the buildings to the public, began in 1793. French kings often used the Louvre to store works of art. Napoleon, after warring in Italy, the Netherlands and Germany, put the art treasures he took as plunder in the Louvre. A great number of these were later returned, but many are still there.

From the Champs Elysée, crossing the Place de la Concorde, once the Place de la Révolution where the guillotine worked so long with such gruesome efficiency, the very air of this part of Paris seems to vibrate with the tumult the great square has witnessed in its long existence.

Jean-François had very little money, and unless he managed to sell some of his literary work he would have to be extremely careful. Thus far he had had no success in finding any sort of a position that would give him an income. He began to realize that marriage was out of the question. Jean-Jacques had promised to give him all the help he could, but living was becoming an expensive business for him. Zoë had given birth to a son, whom they called Ali Champollion-Figeac, to whom Jean-François was godfather. For Jean-Jacques, the most important thing was that his younger brother have this chance to know the great minds in Paris and study hieroglyphics. Despite his added expenses he continued to help his brother as much as possible.

Jean-François hunted for a place to stay and finally found a tiny room close to the Louvre. It was cheap and rather shabby, but with his slender means it was good enough. At the top of an old building that probably had once been the home of an aristocrat, it was badly in need of repair and maintenance. In the room there was an iron bed, a rickety sofa and two chairs. There was a cupboard where he could put his clothes, which were few. In the fashion of the day, Jean-François wore a morning coat over narrow trousers. Above the velvet collar of his coat rose the high white collar of his shirt, with which he wore a heavy stock at his throat.

Monsieur Sylvestre de Sacy, a most sincere and kindly

man, was a dedicated scholar. He had been raised by his widowed mother and trained for the civil service. He became a councilor at the Cour des Monnaies, a court that handled civil suits. His experiences at this court, and the many human problems he faced, had taught de Sacy to become a good businessman. In addition to this, he had mastered all the Semitic languages. He never ceased his studies while he worked as a civil servant, and had built himself a great reputation as an orientalist.

Monsieur de Sacy was a good Catholic, and when the revolution came, being also a confirmed royalist, he retired from his office. He felt that he could not serve the Republic with a clear conscience. The result of this decision was that teaching and oriental study claimed him wholly. A member of the august Academy of Inscriptions, he was given the post of professor of Arabic in the newly established School of Living Eastern Languages.

Shortly after he took up his new post in 1792, Monsieur de Sacy was asked to take an oath of hatred for royalty. He refused and offered his resignation. His reputation as a good and honest man was so high, however, that no further action was taken against him and he was allowed to go on teaching in peace. Napoleon made him a baron and he was also a founder of the Société Asiatique. Although he was famous, de Sacy was always readily available to anyone who sought his advice. He was forty-nine years old when Jean-Jacques made the introduction for his brother.

"Ah yes, I find your comments upon hieroglyphic cartouches and the demotic names you have read very encouraging for my own work, Monsieur de Sacy," Jean-François said.

Monsieur de Sacy was not a pompous man, but he had become accustomed to being met with a rather awed respect from people he did not know. He was somewhat taken aback by the apparent brashness of this seventeen-year-old youth who had just been introduced to him. Yet he quickly saw that Jean-François did not intend to be rude. The young man was just utterly absorbed by the subject of ancient Egypt.

"Reading the demotic and Greek texts from the Rosetta Stone will not, apparently, make it any easier for us to decipher the hieroglyphs, will it?" Jean-François went on. "It is my opinion that we must try to find symbolic, religious meaning in them first. I have found nothing so far to suggest to me that an alphabet might be hidden in them. I am convinced," Jean-François said, "that some form of Coptic must have been spoken by the ancient Egyptians. Monsieur de Sacy, why has it not been possible to decipher more of the demotic script?"

Monsieur de Sacy's smile faded and a frown took its place. He looked thoughtfully at Jean-François. From time to time he had heard Fourier and others mention the brilliant young man from Grenoble. Though skillful himself, Monsieur de Sacy was awed at the amount of energy this young fellow used to master so many languages. The lad knew many more than he did. De Sacy was captivated by the handsome linguist less than half his own age. He could not recall ever meeting anyone with so much self-assurance.

"I confess, young man, that it seems beyond my powers

to go further. You see, there are some signs in the script which appear to be totally at odds with the rest of it. Perhaps someone like yourself will have better luck."

Before Jean-François could interrupt, de Sacy went on. "By the way, your brother sent me a copy of the paper you read to the faculty at Grenoble. Most interesting. Frankly, I think you may well have set yourself an impossible task. If not that, then certainly it is going to take you a lifetime to prepare such a study. We know so very little about Egypt even today, let alone of the time of the pharaohs."

"I do not think so," Jean-François asserted. "In fact, I have already gathered a great deal of material for the book." He continued to explain to de Sacy how he intended to describe the geography of the two kingdoms, Upper and Lower Egypt. He spoke of his work on the chronology of the dynasties and how he intended to show the political and religious structure of the ancient civilization.

Soon after, through de Sacy, Jean-François met many of the greatest minds in Paris. Such exalted company intoxicated him, but he managed to maintain a sense of proportion even though he knew he was widely discussed. Sometimes he was homesick for the beauty of Grenoble, and sometimes thoughts of Pauline distracted him, making it hard to concentrate. But, for the most part, he succeeded in keeping these troubles out of his mind.

Jean-François often ate rapidly and sparingly. He sought out small establishments where he could buy bread which he sometimes ate with a piece of cheese and an onion. Sometimes he could afford a bowl of stew. Feast days came when he received an invitation to dinner from one or another of the men he knew.

There were hard days ahead. None of the well-placed men he had met had been able to help him secure a position. He nursed his money, fearful to reveal how hard pressed he really was. Sometimes he went hungry but tried to ignore it. The gray dampness that some days hung like a pall over Paris affected him and he developed a bad cough, with sometimes severe spasms.

In Paris, oddly enough, Jean-François appeared temporarily to put aside his effort to translate hieroglyphics. He continued to concentrate on oriental languages, seeking to discover their development and what possible connections there might be between them. He had a notion that possibly they had a common origin and had grown from ancient Coptic.

Jean-François's mastery of Arabic was so perfect that one day, at a gathering, a group of Arabs saluted him. They had taken it for granted, because of his looks and fluent use of their tongue, that he was one of them! They were astonished to discover that he was a Frenchman who had never been out of France! On another occasion he was having a discussion with a man who was famous for his travels in the little-known African countries. This man knew Egypt very well.

"*Bon Dieu!*" exclaimed Somini de Manencourt. "You know the country as well as I do myself. It is incredible. I can scarcely believe that you have never set foot in Egypt."

Though he was becoming very well known in Paris, Jean-François still could not find a position. Perhaps his youth worked against him. He could not even find any work tutoring privately. As he worked on his book he began to reconsider his private life. Was he falling out of love with Pauline? Had he ever *really* been in love with her? He found it hard now to conjure up a mental image of her. Jean-François despaired until he accepted the hopelessness of his situation. There could be no future with Pauline.

As usual, once he had made up his mind, Jean-François went to the heart of the matter. With the directness that people often took for rudeness and tactlessness, he abruptly broke his engagement. "It is obvious," he wrote, "that some years must pass before I can afford marriage. I consider it best that this affair end swiftly and cleanly rather than allow it to degenerate into feelings of bitterness."

Pauline, who was not feeling well at the time, was more than usually upset when she got the news. Her parents were disgusted with Jean-François, refusing to understand his reasoning. They bitterly resented his action and his interference in the life of their daughter, an interference which they had tried to prevent. However, there was nothing they could do other than bow to the inevitable.

Breaking his engagement did nothing to lift Jean-François's spirits. Pauline proved herself to be understanding and made no recriminations. In fact, they stayed friends for the rest of what was to be her short life.

Jean-François's money was dwindling at an alarming rate. He could barely scrape together enough to pay his rent, little though it was. So shabby had he become, he was too embarrassed to appear in public and turned into a hermit for a time. Lack of proper nourishment and the demands he made upon his store of energy weakened him more than he knew. Finally, all his money gone, he was forced to write to his brother.

"I am beside myself," he wrote, "and I don't know where to turn next. My shoes are worn through, my shirts are in rags. I am ashamed to appear in public, I look so ragged."

Jean-Jacques replied that he would have to pawn his library in order to help his brother. He urged him to cut expenses still further, not really understanding that Jean-François was in truly desperate straits. That winter was a very hard one. Jean-François's room was cold and damp. His coughing spells grew worse and more frequent. He stuffed paper in his shoes, for his soles had gone, but his feet still got wet. Inevitably, he got sick. Sometimes the pains in his chest were excruciating.

As if he did not have troubles enough, an edict was issued by the Emperor Napoleon ordering conscription for all males over sixteen years of age, making them liable for military service.

Jean-François did not share all his brother's enthusiasm for Napoleon. He clung to his own ideas of what constituted real freedom. Napoleon had not become the benevolent totalitarian ruler Jean-François had once thought he might possibly become. Here was more proof of the warring tyrant he really was. Jean-François was filled with dismay. He could not imagine becoming an insignificant cog in a military machine dedicated to the glory of the emperor. The thought of such a life appalled him. He could not stop his search for knowledge now, and there would be precious little chance of pursuing his studies in the army.

Jean-François could make great sacrifices for the things he cared about and believed in, but this was too much. Despairingly he wrote to Jean-Jacques for advice and help.

"I don't know what to do. I don't want to disappear into the nameless military. There are days," he went on, "when I almost lose my head!"

Jean-Jacques wrote letters to important people. He sought and won the aid of friends who drew up a petition arguing the sound reasons why a scholar like Jean-François should be left to continue his studies. Monsieur de Sacy brought his influence to bear for the sake of Jean-François's researches. Fourier helped. They pointed out that the brilliant young man would be far more useful to France as a teacher. Eventually, these efforts were successful. He was exempted from military service.

It was strange, since the inscriptions of the Rosetta Stone had been such a powerful pull to Paris, that Jean-François skirted around it rather than going right to his self-appointed task of deciphering the hieroglyphs on the stone slab. But, in 1808, a new plaster copy, made in London from the original, reached Paris. Until this time, Jean-François had still believed he was not yet properly equipped for his task. Now, contemplating the new copy of the Rosetta Stone inscriptions, he could no longer resist.

By late August he was able to write to his brother at Grenoble, "I believe I have found the correct values for a whole row of letters from the stele. I submit my first step to you for your examination." He was just eighteen years old, yet he knew with all his soul that he had made the right start.

At this very instant of first success, Jean-François learned of a terrible threat. He was on his way to the Collège de France when, on the street, he met a friend.

"Have you heard the news, François?" his friend inquired.

"What news is that?" he asked.

"Alexander Lenoir has deciphered the hieroglyphs! His book is just out and he calls it *Nouvelles Explications* [New Explanations]!"

Jean-François thought he was going to faint. Pale and gasping, he hung on to a post at the edge of the curb. His heart pounded.

"That is strange," he said finally. "Only yesterday I saw Lenoir and he said nothing about it." Jean-François had known Lenoir for some months. But, decipher hieroglyphs? It just could not be, for Lenoir simply did not have the imagination for such a task. Jean-François realized in that moment just how much it had meant to him all these years he had been preparing to decipher hieroglyphics. It had not occurred to him that someone else might do it first. If he had been beaten to it—his life would hold no purpose.

"No," he said, "it's impossible! Such a task is quite beyond Lenoir's ability!"

"But I have seen it!" his friend insisted. "Why is it impossible? It is only natural Lenoir would remain quiet about it until he was ready to publish."

Jean-François dashed away from his friend to the nearest bookstore. Still breathless, he paid the few francs for what was hardly more than a pamphlet, snatched it up and ran

114

back to his room. He sat down immediately and started reading Lenoir's "new explanations."

Down below, the concierge was startled. Hysterical laughter, dreadful howls and moans were coming from Jean-François's room. With a horrified look on her face, the concierge heaved her bulk into motion and ran to Jean-François's room as fast as she could manage. She pushed open the door. He was rolling about the room, his hands pressed to his stomach. The concierge thought he must be having a fit. "Monsieur Champollion," she cried, "whatever is wrong with you? Are you ill? Shall I call a doctor?"

"Pardon, Madame," he said, wiping the tears from his face. "It's nothing, just a huge joke. I am sorry if I startled you. I assure you I am quite well."

Nevertheless, Jean-François had been badly shaken. He shook his head in silent disbelief. Poor Lenoir had fallen victim, as had so many others, to the frantic guessing game of hieroglyphics. Lenoir must have taken leave of his senses! He had lost all sense of proportion! Now Jean-François could relax and enjoy the joke. Lenoir's "new explanations" was a conglomeration of fantasy and guesswork, well larded with free invention.

That night, ghostly Egyptian voices spoke to Jean-François in a dream. They assured him that he would succeed, that all would be well. But he never forgot the moment when he first thought he had been beaten in the struggle to decipher hieroglyphics.

CHAPTER 8

NAPOLEON RETURNS

In Paris, Jean-François's small means were almost exhausted. Fortunately, in 1809, he was called back to Grenoble to accept the post of professor of history at the university. Shortly after his brother's return, Jean-Jacques accepted the post of librarian at the Imperial Library in Paris and moved to the capital. Jean-François saw Pauline occasionally when she visited Zoë before the move to Paris. He met, and became interested in a cousin of Zoë's, Rosine Blanc.

Perhaps it is inevitable that a young man as brilliant as Jean-François would have some detractors. Older professors felt humiliated at the younger man's rapid elevation. They felt they had been by-passed, their long experience overlooked. They failed to take into account that Jean-François's qualifications were much superior to their own. For all their seniority, how many could claim to have accomplished as much as the young Professor Champollion. More than anyone else, these disgruntled educators should have realized that age alone is not sufficient basis for judging a man's abilities. But jealousy and fair play cannot live in harmony, and some of these men joined hands.

"It is ridiculous," they complained. "Where is this book he's supposed to produce? He got his position solely on an *outline* of it. But where's the book?"

"Champollion is scarcely more than a boy! Why he's barely finished his days as a student. How can one so young have the ability and experience to teach boys his own age and older?"

"The situation is ludicrous," said another professor. "This young man of no experience is permitted to enjoy the same prestige and salary as those of us who have slaved for years to reach our positions! I think we should take our complaint to the lyceum administrators!"

Zoë learned of the complaints and gossip before she left for Paris with Jean-Jacques. She tried to warn Jean-François that trouble was brewing.

"There is a small clique of professors banding together against you. They are determined to force you from the faculty," she warned. "I don't understand why, but it seems that you go out of your way to antagonize them. They are old men who have lived through troubled times. You cannot change men like that who are set in their ways. Pointing out errors in their instruction, telling them they are hypocritical, can hardly endear you to them. Sagîr, these teachers resent a young man like you being raised to a position above them. Why can't you leave them to their own devices and concentrate on your own work?"

Jean-François shrugged. "I do not like to compromise with truth. They are pompous know-nothings," he retorted. "They have no interest in truth and it is shameful to play politics with education. They find it easy to hide truth and teach whatever they feel will please the government, whether that be king, emperor or republic! Just look at the grief our country has endured. And these men stand by without raising a voice in protest. It is too much!"

Nevertheless, living with the knowledge of the unfairness of those who attacked him, Jean-François became embittered and moody. He missed Zoë and Jean-Jacques and, being unwelcome at the Berriat home, he saw little of Pauline. Except for those times he saw Rosine, he was very lonely.

As a result of the pressure from his detractors, Jean-François was forced to accept a big cut in his salary. It was an empty triumph of malicious ignorance, but it seemed to pacify Jean-François's disgruntled colleagues for a while. He complained bitterly of this and of being overburdened with work that was rightfully the task of others. He complained, too, that he was not being paid the proper fees for work he did, but to no avail.

Though very outspoken in his views, Jean-François was not a supporter of any party. He was imprudent, which made it easy for those who disliked him to give his remarks political connotations to suit their own purposes. He refused to teach history in a way that would please Napoleon's administrators, whom he regarded as pandering lackeys. Nor would he try to win favor with the Bourbons. For him only truth mattered. To find truth, teachers had to be intellectually free and immune from pressure.

His enemies found it easy to live with compromise. They had no objection to flattering the emperor. They could just as easily flatter the Bourbons when it was politically necessary. Such an attitude disgusted Jean-François and he was disliked all the more for expressing his views. Satirical songs and small plays began to be heard in the salons and streets of Grenoble. Though he did not put his name to them, there were those who suspected this was the handiwork of Jean-François. There were moments, after the blow of his reduction in salary, when he grew discouraged. He wrote to Jean-Jacques:

"My lot is decided. I must be poor as Diogenes. I must try to buy myself a barrel to live in and sacking to wear on my back. Then perhaps I can hope to subsist on the well-known generosity of the Athenians."

But discouragements passed. He stonily ignored his critics, knowing them for the small souls they were. Let them pamper the regime of Napoleon!

Jean-François, again not signing them, began to write satires on the emperor and those who served him and the politics of the time. Generally he would take themes from classic Greek plays such as Euripides' *Iphigenia in Tauris*. Nobody openly accused him of being the author of these satires and, fortunately, these attacks were too mild to reach the ears of the emperor. These small assaults upon authority, however, occupied only a small part of Jean-François's time. Most of his attention went into the compilations of his Coptic dictionary when he was not teaching.

Napoleon wanted an heir. He divorced the childless Josephine and, in April 1810, married Archduchess Marie Louisa of Austria. This alliance would also, with the Austro-Hungarian Empire neutralized, leave him free to deal with

England. When a son was born to Napoleon and Marie Louisa, Napoleon made the child King of Rome.

In September, 1812, leading an army of 600,000 men, Napoleon invaded Russia. By December, after an ignoble retreat from Moscow, his army had been reduced to 120,000 men. Marshal Ney covered the rearguard on the awful retreat in the bitterly cold winter. Austria, Russia and Prussia now joined against Napoleon. He was defeated at Leipzig and forced back within the borders of France. His enemies pursued him into France and on April 11, 1814, Napoleon was forced to abdicate and was exiled to the island of Elba in the Mediterranean, off the coast of Italy. The Bourbons reclaimed the French throne.

Taking note of these incredible events, Jean-François took time to write another anonymous and popular satire. In this work, which he called "Departure of the Eagle—Return of the Lily" (the Bourbon fleur de lys), several saints, including a character he called Saint Napoleon, engage in debate. One dialogue takes place between a despotic Asian ruler and a European king; the king makes clear to the Asian despot the dangers of constitutional government. Jean-François, in this satire, makes his own view clear that neither of these characters discussing so "wisely" the condition of the world was fit to rule over free men.

By this same year, the paper that Jean-François had read to the faculty in 1807 had become a two-volume study. When it was published in 1814, Jean-François was just twenty-four years old. The volumes, *Egypt Under the Pharaohs*, created a furor. Though there were those who dismissed it as ridiculous fantasy, others praised it and saw its true value. There could be no doubting that Jean-François was one of the brightest stars in the new science of Egyptology.

He was, though, quite wrong in many of his conclusions. This was especially so of the chronology of the pharaohs. Considering the scrappy sources upon which he had worked so hard, and that the remains of ancient Egypt had not yet been uncovered by the archaeologist's shovel, it was a remarkable performance. It provided scholars with a framework around which to build the body of their science.

As Jean-François pointed out, "It is a beginning. Where there are gaps in our knowledge, they can be filled. Where the chronology is inaccurate, it can be corrected as we learn more of the pharaohs. Let those who criticize turn their attention to these matters."

Since recognition was now his, Jean-François's enemies were even more envious. They made it a point to spread once more the tale of how he had torn down the lily banner and replaced it with the tricolor. It had been a passion of the moment, a boyish blow for freedom which he had hoped was to come with the rule of Napoleon.

In terms of present knowledge, Jean-François's study of ancient Egypt could not be called definitive. Far too little was known about the country for that. Nevertheless, publication of *Egypt Under the Pharaohs* set the seal on the quality of his research and eased his financial situation considerably.

The young scholar now devoted all the time he could to deciphering hieroglyphics. Few scholars were aware yet how much progress he had made, for he was not ready to reveal it, but he felt very sure that he had found the correct value for at least a dozen symbols. He admitted that he had been wrong, along with many others, in giving so much consideration to religious meaning in the hieroglyphs. Now he knew beyond doubt that the symbols were, indeed, a language. But he would need more than a dozen interpretations before he could feel secure enough to announce the result of his work.

Napoleon was treated very well by the allies who defeated him, and by his own country for the most part. He was given sovereignty of the island of Elba and allowed to keep the title of emperor. He was also granted a revenue of two million francs, about $500,000 today. He traveled into exile with several of his aides and four members of the commission who had signed the treaty with him at Fontainebleau.

There were angry and violent demonstrations against him by royalists during his journey. At Avignon, his carriage was stopped by a mob. Momentarily, it looked as though Napoleon was fated to die at their hands, but he was allowed to proceed. All along his route he was jeered, saw himself hanged in effigy, listened to shouts of "coward" and was spat upon by many who not long before had cheered him.

These memories troubled him at Elba. His mother, who was with him in exile, often taunted him. "Fulfill your destiny," she would insist. "My son, you were not meant to die on this island." He made his mind up to escape from

Elba by January 1815. An aide had come to Elba reporting that the Bourbons were weak and unpopular with many Frenchmen. Napoleon still had powerful friends in France. In February, the British commissioner who was guarding Napoleon for England, Sir Neil Campbell, left Elba for a visit to Italy.

Napoleon had no fear of the returned Bourbons. During the Revolution, Louis XVIII had held court at Coblenz, in Germany. When he fled France, he had proclaimed his nephew, the son of his brother Louis XVI, king. Louis XVII died while a prisoner in Paris and Louis XVIII, his uncle, succeeded to the title. Napoleon knew he had every chance of re-establishing his regime in France.

While Sir Neil Campbell was away, Napoleon ordered the one warship he had left fitted out and provisioned. When Campbell returned to Elba he discovered that Napoleon had sailed two days before, the twenty-sixth of February. It was too late for any English ship to overtake Napoleon's *Inconstant*. Actually, the *Inconstant* eluded both English and French warships who did not suspect her identity. On March 1, 1815, Napoleon landed, unopposed, at Antibes, in the South of France.

Remembering his experiences at the hands of the royalists in Provence, Napoleon decided to avoid that province as much as he could. There was a sizable garrison at Grenoble and, if Napoleon could win them over, he felt sure he would reach Paris without having to fire a shot. The Dauphinois had always been enthusiastic toward him. He chose a route (now called Route Napoleon) through the lower Alps which took him through Grasse, Digne and on to Grenoble.

The route was difficult—a rough, winding road marked by immense outcroppings of bare rock and dotted with enormous stands of pine on hillsides too steep to pasture or cultivate. Patches of alpine rose, a dwarf rhododendron, glowed bright red and pink almost to the edge of the snow line of the mountains. The air was crisp and the spirits of Napoleon's soldiers were high.

Napoleon and his few soldiers slowly trudged along the foothills of the Maritime Alps, climbing steadily upward toward the snow-capped heights. Spring was early and the clear air bore the scent of a profusion of wild flowers growing in the cattle-dotted meadows. On past laboriously terraced, steep, vine-covered slopes the small army marched.

News of the escape reached Paris on March 5 and there was immediate, frantic activity in the capital. Newspaper headlines screamed of Napoleon's escape, describing him as "monster," "tyrant"; in a despicably short time new headlines were stating "His Majesty Approaches Paris!" An army was sent to capture Napoleon. This army was commanded by Marshal Ney, the very man who had been one of Napoleon's favorites and served him so well in Russia before the emperor's downfall. This Prince of Moskwa, a title earned during the Russian campaign, now served the king and promised that he would bring his late emperor back to Paris *in an iron cage!*

Napoleon had a few less than a thousand soldiers, including some Polish lancers, as he approached Grenoble. Descending the mountains into the beautiful Isère valley, he found his way barred by a regiment of infantry. Ordering his men to trail arms, Napoleon advanced alone. "Shoot your emperor if you wish," he called to the soldiers barring his way. Instead, ignoring the commands of their officers, the men broke ranks and, shouting *Vive l'Empereur*, surrounded the easily recognized figure in the long gray coat. Napoleon had won! He learned that an old aide of his was in command of the garrison at Grenoble and his optimism was boundless. The garrison would surely join him.

It was evening, March 7, when the city gates were reached. Torchlight dramatically picked out Napoleon's features. Calmly he looked up at the guns pointing toward him. Men were aimlessly running about on the walls. Advancing alone, under the menacing guns, Napoleon took a pinch of snuff and tapped upon the gate with the silver snuff box. There was a momentary, deadly silence. Then, suddenly, in surging waves came the roaring cheer of *Vive l'Empereur!* Napoleon had conquered again!

At last Napoleon's path was to cross that of the Champollions.

Jean-Jacques, who was in Grenoble, was overjoyed by these events. He was even more excited when the mayor of Grenoble sent for him.

"Professor Champollion," the mayor said, "a wonderful opportunity has come your way. The emperor has asked me to find a suitable man to be his secretary. There isn't anybody I would recommend in preference to you so I have given the emperor your name. There is one thing I had better tell you," the mayor said with a chuckle. "The emperor is very susceptible to omens, as you may know. I decided on a little ruse quite deliberately. I misspelled your name and to the emperor you are Professor Champoleon!

The emperor was charmed. 'Ah, a good omen,' he said to me. 'He has half my own name!' "

Jean-Jacques grinned and thanked the mayor for recommending him for the post.

"You will be sent for shortly," the mayor replied. "Hold yourself in readiness and don't forget the new spelling of your name!"

Jean-François accompanied his brother when he went to be interviewed by Napoleon. Napoleon was unaware that the younger brother had lampooned him. He knew nothing of the satires, and Jean-François, though his manner was aloof, conceded that Napoleon was a most compelling personality. In the uncertainty of what was happening, Jean-François's enemies kept silent.

Napoleon was deeply impressed by the handsome young professor. Sweet memories of his own successes in Egypt returned as they talked. Napoleon was full of questions about Jean-François's studies, and amazed at his knowledge of Egypt. After browsing through *Egypt Under the Pharaohs*, Napoleon, too, found it hard to believe Jean-François had never been to Egypt. This young teacher had conquered Egypt in a way very different from his own triumphs there. Together, the Champollions and Napoleon chuckled over Jean-Jacques's failure to secure a place with the expedition. "Later, we must see what we can do to correct that error," Napoleon said.

After he had listened to Jean-François describe the progress he was making with his Coptic dictionary, Napoleon made a grand gesture to the young man.

"When I return to Paris," the emperor said, "I shall see to

it that your dictionary is published at government expense. When I have established my authority once more in France, I think, Professor Champollion, we may again do great things in Egypt. I shall have need of you."

Jean-François thanked the emperor for his kindness and, bowing, the brothers withdrew from Napoleon's presence.

So fascinated was Napoleon with Jean-François that the next day he called upon him at the university library. So different these two men, the scholar and the soldier, but they had one thing in common, a spirit of daring and great imagination.

Napoleon wanted to talk more about Egypt and his future plans for that country.

"Once Egypt is again conquered," he exclaimed, "I shall create great irrigation projects. The earth is rich and I shall make it bloom. In this way I shall restore prosperity and wealth to the country." Napoleon gazed at Jean-François thoughtfully. "The main purpose of my visit to you today is that I have made a decision. Using your dictionary as a basis, I intend to restore Coptic as the official language of Egypt." He glanced at Jean-François, seeking his reaction, but Jean-François's serious expression gave no clue to his thoughts. "You must not fail to be ready when I send for you. The time is not far off," Napoleon concluded.

Jean-François related the talk he had had with Napoleon to his brother.

"Let us hope then that all goes well for the emperor in his march on Paris," Jean-Jacques commented. "I am to accompany him when the troops start out. He is taking the garrison from Grenoble, which gives him an army to be reckoned with I think. These are exciting days," Jean-Jacques said with enthusiasm. "I feel good to be alive and the future is bright with promise."

Jean-François was skeptical. "Perhaps," he said. "But I doubt it. History teaches, and Napoleon himself has proved that, when a man holds the final power, the power of life and death, in his hands, he changes. The bright promise is lost, the cherished ideals become tarnished."

"Well," said Jean-Jacques, "we shall soon see which of us is right."

Though he was a brilliant soldier, Marshal Ney was a simple family man. When he came within sight of the old tricolor under which he had served Napoleon for so long, he could not resist the appeal of the flag or sympathy with his old emperor's cause, so Marshal Ney took his army over to Napoleon's side.

Louis XVIII once more fled France.

At Ligny, on June 16, Napoleon defeated the Prussian army, led by Blucher. At Waterloo, south of Brussels, Napoleon had 124,000 men to oppose Wellington's combined forces of English, Dutch, Belgian and Hanoverian soldiers. For a while it appeared that Napoleon was winning, but Blucher hurried to reinforce Wellington with the remainder of his forces collected after the battle of Ligny. It angered Napoleon to see the Prussians join his opponent. After a battle lasting six hours Napoleon saw his large army destroyed and his hopes of regaining France disappear. His defeat was a total one, and by June 22 Napoleon was again exiled. This time he was sent to the island of St. Helena in the lonely south Atlantic. Wisely, perhaps remembering Joan of Arc, the British spared his life once more. The hopes of The Hundred Days were shattered.

Any expectations Jean-François may have had from Napoleon's promises now evaporated. The Bourbons returned and immediately began the horrors of the White Terror. Blood flowed as thousands were arrested and executed. Marshal Ney was arrested and on December 5, 1815, was executed by a firing squad in the gardens of the Luxembourg in Paris.

For his attachment to and other "traitorous" activities for Napoleon, Jean-Jacques lost his post at the Imperial Library. He was fortunate enough to secure another post immediately, accepting the responsibility for the huge library at the palace of Fontainebleau. Jean-Jacques was happy enough to move the thirty-five miles from Paris to his new position, which he kept for the rest of his life.

Royalist troops approached Grenoble, but there was no garrison to defend the town, since they had gone with Napoleon. Jean-François went to join the men on the city walls who were attempting to protect Grenoble. He was no soldier, but he intended to do his part for freedom. There was little organization, much milling about and general confusion among the defenders. The moment General Latour opened his bombardment of the town, Jean-François fled, but not because he was a coward. Fires broke out and Jean-François panicked with fear for his precious manuscripts at the lyceum library. He raced to the lyceum and spent the rest of the day dashing about with buckets of sand and water dousing fires that threatened the library.

Jean-François had made a bad error in judgment. Though he did not follow Napoleon, his brother had, and his enemies made the most of it. He did something, too, which would not likely endear him to the Bourbons. Because of his dislike of autocratic rule, Jean-François had given his name and assistance in founding The Delphinatic League. The aim of this organization was the promotion of liberty and freedom for all men everywhere. The organization and the men who founded it could hardly expect to find favor with the Bourbon regime.

The downfall of Napoleon brought misery for Jean-François in its wake. Though it was not proved that he was their author, Jean-François's satires poked fun at the Bourbons, as well as Napoleon. There was a good deal of gossiping about this fact. The young professor feared Bourbon revenge for his activities and his enemies were not reluctant to recount, for the benefit of the Bourbon administration at the lyceum, the incident of his tearing down the lily banner. Though not arrested, he was openly accused of being a traitor! He was suspended from the university and not permitted to teach. The suspension lasted eighteen months.

Jean-François retaliated by loudly declaring his belief in intellectual freedom. Smothered by countless petty royalist restrictions, his enemies were gradually wearing him down. To a friend one day, Jean-François quoted from the *Zend-Avesta*, a holy book of the Parsees of India, "Make your fields arable! It is better to make six acres of poor land arable than it is to win twenty-four battles!" He echoed, "That, too, is my opinion!"

The cessation of teaching assignments proved to be a good thing. Occasionally he called upon Rosine Blanc, but apart from this he withdrew from political activity and concentrated his whole attention upon the translation of hieroglyphics.

CHAPTER 9

"CLEOPATRA'S NEEDLE"

Despite his withdrawal, whisperings of his "traitorous activities" grew more menacing now that the Bourbons had regained control of France. Sickened by the circumstances of his present existence in Grenoble and seeing no prospects of regaining his post at the lyceum, Jean-François quietly left Grenoble for Paris. He visited Rosine Blanc briefly before leaving.

Since the time of the Roman Empire, Italy had possessed several enormous stone obelisks that had been brought from Egypt. It is strange indeed that, until the time of Napoleon's expedition, very little real attention had been paid them. All of them were inscribed, but nothing was known about the meaning of the inscriptions. As more statuary, inscribed antiquities and papyri reached the scholars in Europe for study, these great stone monuments were given closer scrutiny.

The Obelisk of Seti I, which stands in the Piazza del Popolo in Rome, is seventy-eight feet high and weighs 235 tons. Originally, it had been set up at Heliopolis, near Cairo, about 1300 B.C. It was taken to Rome by the Emperor Augustus about 23 B.C., and set up in the Circus Maximus. Augustus dedicated it to the sun and the commemoration of the Roman conquest of Egypt. At some time after the fall of Rome, the obelisk had toppled over on its side. It lay buried in ruins until the time of Pope Sixtus V. He ordered Domenico Fontana to set the obelisk in its present position in 1589.

Seti I died before the inscriptions he had ordered carved on the obelisk were finished. It is now known that the work was completed by his son, Ramses II.

Italy has several other very fine specimens of obelisks, and others are, today, set up in Paris, London, New York and Washington, and other cities.

It was an obelisk that finally provided Jean-François the means to decipher accurately the hieroglyphic script.

Frederic Caillaird, a goldsmith by trade, but a very intelligent man who seemed to thrive on travel and adventure, was traveling in Egypt. On the island of Philae, in the river Nile near Aswan, he found an obelisk. Caillaird copied the inscriptions from it and circulated them among the scholars in Paris.

This obelisk was smaller than most, being twenty-two feet high and weighing six tons. It had been shifted from the island after Caillaird found it, but nobody in Egypt seemed to want it until it was sold to Mr. William Bankes. Mr. Bankes shipped it to his estate in Dorsetshire, England, in 1821.

With the man who had finally defeated Napoleon looking on, the Duke of Wellington, Mr. Bankes had the obelisk set up in his park at Kingston Lacey. On the base of this obelisk had been found an inscription in Greek which made the obelisk practically a second Rosetta Stone. There were several cartouches among the inscribed hieroglyphs on it. Jean-François had seen copies of these inscriptions and from these had started his serious effort to decipher the peculiar signs.

Perhaps because hers was one of the first names read from it, and no doubt because of the romance and glamor that her name always evoked, the British promptly dubbed their obelisks "Cleopatra's Needles." The most famous and celebrated of these stands on the embankment of the river Thames, not very far from the Houses of Parliament. When this obelisk was set in place, Queen Victoria's name, in hieroglyphs, was also carved upon it. The term "Cleopatra's Needles" still clings, although in many cases the inscriptions on these obelisks have nothing to do with the Egyptian queen.

In 1814, the year Jean-François published his study *Egypt Under the Pharaohs*, a man in England announced some of the results of his attempts to decipher the demotic script, working from the Rosetta Stone in the British Museum.

Dr. Thomas Young was a well known and widely respected scientist, a naturalist, *not* a philologist. Nevertheless, like many scholars of the day with other specializations, Dr. Young became fascinated by the newly discovered wonders of ancient Egypt. He was one of the men who steadfastly believed that hieroglyphics must contain symbolic signs *and* alphabetical characters like those discovered by Akerblad in the demotic script. Dr. Young claimed to have read the

135

names of Ptolemy and Berenice from hieroglyphs, but he did not show how he had done this. He concentrated at first chiefly upon the demotic script of the Rosetta Stone. The comments he made upon the value of the signs within cartouches, and their importance, did not escape Jean-François's attention. However, that was about the only clue that he provided the French scholar.

Dr. Young's place in the science of Egyptology is a very honored and respected one. First, he learned the ancient Coptic language and adopted Akerblad's alphabet. He *did*, from the start, suspect that the demotic script contained symbolic signs as well as letters. These were the signs that had frustrated the efforts of Monsieur de Sacy and others. Dr. Young compared groups of characters in demotic with their equivalents in Greek. Thus the names of Alexander and Alexandria, which occur in the fourth and fourteenth lines of the Greek script, he placed in the second and tenth lines of the demotic script. He noticed the occurrence, in practically every line of the script, of a grouping of signs that he felt might signify a period or a common particle. Eventually these groupings were found to be the equivalent of the English conjunction *and*.

Next, Dr. Young noticed a collection of outstanding characters that occurred thirty times in the demotic script. On comparing with the Greek text, he found the Greek word for king. From this he translated the groupings by that word. Again he compared the number of times this grouping occurred in both demotic and Greek texts.

Young's next step was to write the Greek text over the demotic in such a way that what he believed were coincident words would be juxtaposed. In this manner the intermediate parts of the two texts were brought nearer together and the area of comparison was considerably narrowed. From this method Dr. Young found nineteen letters discovered by Akerblad and twelve more of his own, besides a star at the end of proper names. He found fifty groups of words, including those already found by Monsieur de Sacy. He added one hundred and fifty more letters from the demotic script for which he thought he had found Greek equivalents. But it later proved he was often wrong.

The puzzle that plagued Dr. Young and his contemporaries was the few symbolic signs in the demotic script for which they could find no meaning. For all its limitations, it was Dr. Young's contribution to understanding that led finally to successful decipherment of the hieroglyphs.

Being a man of courage and great integrity, Jean-François was not afraid to say, "I am wrong." It was the inscriptions from Mr. Bankes' obelisk that first showed him that he had been going in the wrong direction in his study of hieroglyphics. He, too, had thought the characters might have only symbolic religious meaning. Now he began to think differently.

Jean-François Champollion set out on paths with nothing to guide him except the theories about the importance of the cartouches in deciphering hieroglyphics. His steps were slow and toilsome, but he was certain now that hieroglyphics was the most ancient form of Egyptian writing.

It was something new to have found Cleopatra's name in Greek on the base of Mr. Bankes' obelisk. The name Ptolemy, within a cartouche, was already familiar and Jean-

François noticed among the inscriptions from the small obelisk a similar cartouche. He suspected at once that another, slightly larger cartouche, must contain the name of Cleopatra, for this name appeared in Greek on the obelisk. There had to be the equivalent in hieroglyphics. Feeling his way slowly toward the truth, his imaginative mind and intuition were working with alacrity. He concluded that the signs within the cartouches were, in some instances, phonetic or alphabetic. But it was one thing to know this with his whole soul, to *know* that he was right, and quite another to prove it in such a way that other men could follow his methods for themselves, making independent evaluations.

Almost as soon as he arrived in the capitol, Jean-François found himself the center of violent controversy. The scholars in Paris were involved in a furor of dissension over the publication of the results of Napoleon's expedition. The British, Germans and others added their voices to the ruckus with their own ideas and translations concerning Egypt. Even enlightened members of the general public were reporting and publishing their ideas and views.

By this time, at least, Jean-François was fully aware of what to expect when he added his own voice to the others, and he would have to face the certain ridicule as best he could. He moved boldly forward, knowing that in time he must prevail because he was right.

This time, in Paris, Jean-François *did* allow some of the city's delights to distract him. He was well known now, and though often short of funds, he frequently attended official functions. At one of these he discovered a side to his nature he had not previously known he possessed.

Madame Louise D. was beautiful, witty and gay when Jean-François met her at a party. Though married to an elderly government official, she was flirtatious and she took an instant liking to the handsome young man who was presented to her. Jean-François was intrigued. He was even more intrigued when, during a private moment of conversation, Louise D. softly suggested a rendezvous. Though an honorable man, and aware that she was married, Jean-François found himself quite unable to resist the blandishments of such a charming creature.

Louise D. flitted through life like a brightly colored butterfly, and before he realized the full implications, Jean-François was hopelessly, passionately infatuated with her. Louise D. had no intention of leaving the security her husband provided to form a permanent liaison with the handsome young man she knew was quite poor. But she was equally infatuated with him. The affair drifted for some time, with Jean-François growing more aware all the while that he should bring the impossible situation to an end.

Abruptly, he broke away from Madame Louise D. and returned briefly to Grenoble and more troubles. He had not secured a position during his stay in Paris and there was nothing offered him at Grenoble.

With his usual directness, Jean-François came right to the point of this trip to Grenoble when he called upon Rosine Blanc. He wanted to be married, and perhaps hoped it would help to protect him from the wiles of Louise D.

Rosine and Jean-François, in 1814, became engaged. He was twenty-four years old, she was twenty. Rosine's father, a businessman, was furious when he heard about the engagement.

"What can that young man offer you?" he demanded of his daughter. "You know he is in trouble with the authorities and anything can happen to him. He has no position and, as far as I can discover, no prospects of one."

Rosine timidly reminded her father that Jean-François had recently published a book which was the talk of Paris and Grenoble.

"Bah!" retorted her father. "He won't get fat on what he makes from that! Rosine, I absolutely forbid you to continue this foolish engagement. You are not to see Champollion again!"

But Rosine, a quiet and charming girl, continued to see Jean-François and to write to him secretly. In 1817 Champollion returned to Grenoble and resumed his chair. In 1818 he and Rosine were married, a few months after Pauline Berriat died.

Rosine was shy and quiet and not above average intellectually. She was interested in poetry and music, but in no way accomplished in either art. For her the arts were a diversion, and she was content in the routine of running a middle-class home on limited means. While they lived at Grenoble things went smoothly enough, even though it soon became apparent that Rosine had neither the ability nor the desire to share in her husband's interests. When they went to live in Paris the contrasts of their interests and abilities divided them more sharply.

As his work progressed his interests widened. There was a heady atmosphere among the scholars of Paris, and with them and his brother, Jean-Jacques, to provide all the intellectual stimulation he needed, Jean-François was content. He and Rosine lived together, but she retired more and more into the background and neither one of them seemed to mind it in the least that Rosine became little more than a housekeeper. For many years, whenever he met her at a gathering, Jean-François would go out of his way to avoid Louise D., fearing to become involved with her again. Rosine had the satisfaction, at least, of knowing that her husband was faithful to her.

In 1821, Champollion was once again relieved of his official duties, for political reasons, and once again he went to Paris. By this time Jean-François believed he had sufficient evidence and that he was ready to present his findings to the academic world. Carefully, he set forth his results in what was to become a famous "letter." The paper that he prepared he called, in the fashion of the day, *Letter to Monsieur Dacier in Regard to the Alphabet of the Phonetic Hieroglyphs*. Monsieur Dacier was the permanent secretary of the Academy of Inscriptions in Paris.

Although his "letter" was ready for publication, Jean-François hesitated, waiting a year before delivering it to Monsieur Dacier. And the year 1821 was a most hectic one. Perhaps the knowledge that he was on the verge of alienating a large number of otherwise very fair-minded scholars with the results he had obtained from his hard work caused Jean-François to hesitate. Many fondly held theories and sincere beliefs would be destroyed once his work was known.

Perhaps, too, the death of his father in 1821 distracted him for a time.

This same year, in far-off St. Helena, the man who started it all, with the first organized expedition to Egypt, Napoleon Bonaparte, died.

CHAPTER 10

FUSS AND FUROR

Jean-François was appalled, for, instead of developing, it seemed as though the science of Egyptology was being torn apart. At times he felt as though he was living with madmen. How could serious men offer such opinions and "translations"?

Yet, Jean-François knew why. He, himself, had made the same error in his first approach to hieroglyphics. Far too many researchers still tried to follow the lines indicated by Horapollo. Herodotus (483-425 B.C.), often called the "father of history," still had a great influence on scholars of a later day.

Herodotus traveled in Greece, Egypt, Asia and Scythia and Macedonia. From his travels he produced a book in nine volumes which he named after the nine muses. The second book, which he called *Euterpe* (the muse of Music to the ancient Greeks), is devoted to Egypt. In this work Herodotus recorded what he saw and what explanations he received from Egyptian priests. He included his observations on the manners and customs of the country as well as a list of the succession of the pharaohs. However, he did not claim that the list was chronologically accurate. His work has its greatest value when juxtaposed against other reliable ancient writers. Jean-François, of course, had studied Herodotus.

Strabo (64 B.C.–A.D. 19) was another whose writings confused later scholars. The views of these ancients were believed sound and a worthy basis upon which to make progress. That no progress of any consequence was being made did not seem to concern those who maintained this position.

In Paris it was good for Jean-François to have his brother close. Jean-Jacques advised, edited and made suggestions for the writing his young brother was doing. Though respected by some men, Jean-François was widely mocked and ridiculed for daring to challenge parts of the report of the expedition to Egypt. He challenged on the basis of the expedition's own sketches and comments, but this did nothing to stop the mockery.

In Egypt, at Dendera, on the Nile in Upper Egypt, a great temple in good preservation had been investigated by Napoleon's experts. In this temple was a painted zodiac that had aroused a good deal of curiosity. There was another at a place called Esneh. Jean-François started the controversy over the temple at Dendera by disagreeing with members of the expedition. He had studied their sketches and measurements and given careful attention to their descriptions of the temple. There were some men who claimed the temple was at least 17,000 years old! Many others believed it closer to truth to consider it to be four or five thousand years old. Jean-François disagreed with them all.

The young scholar admitted the beauty of the structure, but he had learned enough about the pharaohs to know that the claims of the temple's age were ridiculously extravagant. He stated his opinion that the building was the work of many pharaohs, and that even Roman emperors had a hand in finishing it. Probably it was not finished until well into the Christian era. With great daring he denied the popular belief that this building was a temple of Isis. He insisted that it was a temple dedicated to the goddess of love and mirth, Hathor.

"No doubt," Jean-François explained, "the confusion arises from the fact that both goddesses are symbolized by sacred cows."

Isis was the wife and sister of Osiris and the mother of Horus. She was the goddess of the moon and of agriculture. The cult of this goddess eventually spread from Memphis to all of Egypt and even Greece and Rome. In human form, Hathor was identified with Aphrodite, the Greek goddess of love and beauty. To the Romans she was Venus.

"Hathor," Jean-François pointed out, "was the goddess of love and mirth. Her sacred cow bears the disc of the sun and also plumes of hawk feathers between its horns. The sketches clearly show Hathor's sacred cow, not that of Isis," he insisted. "Therefore there can be little doubt that the temple was dedicated to her."

For these views, Jean-François was made the laughing stock of Paris. He shrugged off the criticisms, even the vicious ones, and went his own way. He *knew* that he would soon be able to prove his views.

In a patient effort to create some reappraisal of the classic historians, Jean-François focused attention by publishing some comments on the work of Horapollo.

"His work [Horapollo's] is called *Hieroglyphica,* but it does not contain an interpretation of what we know as hieroglyphs. It describes the sacred sculptural symbols, Egyptian emblems which are quite different from real hieroglyphs. Evidence for my idea can be found on Egyptian monuments. The sacred sculptures distinctly show emblematic scenes such as described by Horapollo, the snake biting the swan, the eagle, the heavenly rain, the dove with laurel leaf, etc., but there is nothing emblematic in the real hieroglyphs."

Perhaps in making this effort Jean-François hoped to prepare for the bombshell he was about to drop on the faltering theories of would-be Egyptologists.

The powers of insight and intuition that he possessed are beyond description. He had so thoroughly absorbed the ancient Egyptian's culture into his own being that at times people had an uncanny feeling in his presence that he *was* an ancient Egyptian—reincarnated! His imaginative gifts were great, his approach inspired and he created a sound and practical methodology that other scholars could and did follow with great success.

Dr. Young's approach to the demotic script had been schematic, which meant that, by the use of logic and a preconceived scheme, he hoped to solve the puzzle. Jean-François had prepared himself for his task almost from the first moment he had heard the name of Egypt. Young's results were often no more than inspired guesses—brilliant, but still guesses. He left no real method that other scholars could adopt and follow, and he had made little progress with the hieroglyphic text.

It was Jean-François's mastery of ancient Coptic which led him closer to the spirit of the ancient Egyptian people. He had taken the trouble to master over a dozen dead languages in his efforts to understand the ancient world.

Finally, in 1822, Jean-François was ready to publish his "letter" to Monsieur Dacier. In it he set forth the results of his years of research:

> This first sign in the name of Cleopatra, which represents a kind of quadrant, and which ought to be the letter K (there is no C in Greek) should not occur in the name Ptolemy and it is *not* there. The second, a crouching lion, which should represent the letter L, is identical with the fourth of Ptolemy which is also an L. The third sign is a feather or leaf (stylized reed) which should represent the short vowel E. Two similar leaves may be observed at the end of the name Ptolemy which, by their position, must have the sound of E long. The fourth character to the left, represents a kind of flower or root with its stalk bent downward, and should answer to the letter O, and accordingly the third letter in the name of Ptolemy. The fifth, to the right, is a sort of square, which should represent the letter P, and it is the first in the name of Ptolemy. The sixth, to the left, is a hawk, which should be the letter A. This letter does not occur in the Greek name of Ptolemy, neither does it occur in the hieroglyphic transcription. The seventh is an open hand, representing the T, but this character is not found in the name of Ptolemy, where second letter, T, is expressed by the

segment of a sphere. The eighth sign, a mouth, seen in front, ought to be the letter R, and as that letter does not occur in Ptolemy, it is also absent from his hieroglyphic name. The ninth and last sign, which ought to be the vowel A, is a repetition of the hawk, which has that sign in the sixth. The signs of the feminine on each side of this hawk terminate the name of Cleopatra; that of Ptolemy ends with a bent stalk, which we conclude to be the letter S.

Jean-François knew that the correct spelling of the name was Ptolmis.

Thus, with great insight and ingenuity, he had discovered in the hieroglyphic name of Cleopatra certain signs that, if alphabetical, served to express the letters *k, l, e, o, p, a, t;* and that, if used for the signs of those letters, matched those same signs which occurred in the hieroglyphic name of Ptolemy. These letters could be checked against other names. But there remained the mystery of the two different signs that expressed the letter *t.*

Because of his close attention to the cartouches, Jean-François had discovered twelve letters that could be checked against other inscriptions of hieroglyphics. But how were images of birds, a mouth, an open hand used to express *letters?* This remained to be discovered and explained more fully.

The use of two different signs to express what he believed to be the letter, or sound, *t* continued to intrigue Jean-François. Most scholars might have assumed it wrong to have two signs representing the same letter or sound. Jean-François did not make this mistake. He pondered *why* two different signs represented the same letter and he was certain that both the stylized open hand and the segmented sphere *did* stand for the letter *t*. He instantly saw a probable answer to this puzzle. He thought, supposing the rule by which phonetic value is given to the hieroglyphs is the very simple one of taking either the syllable or initial letter of the word which expressed the name of the thing represented? He decided to probe this possible rule.

Jean-François deduced that the mouth delineated phonetically must be the letter *r*, for the word for mouth was *ro*. An eagle must be *a* because the word for eagle was *akhom*. A hand was *tot;* phonetically, therefore, it became the letter *t*.

Obviously, the names of a great many different objects in hieroglyphics might begin with the same letter, and that letter could be expressed by different signs, either for neatness or ease of writing or perhaps some other cause. But what other cause? Jean-François found his answer. There was a system of homophones embodied in hieroglyphics! Further research revealed to him that this use of homophones was limited to a certain number of objects. The discovery of phonetic signs in the cartouches had led to the discovery of the use of homophones in hieroglyphic writing.

In his analyses of cartouches which gave the names of Ptolemy, (C)Kleopatra, Berenice, Alexander and several Roman emperors, Jean-François explained that vowels were indicated in several ways, and sometimes omitted altogether.

A homophone is a word that is pronounced the same as another with a different meaning, regardless of whether they are spelled alike. Sounds are produced that sound alike —*ks* as in kicks or *x* as in six—but the sounds are used quite differently and in this case different characters are used to make the same sound. So there was nothing really mysterious about having two different signs indicating the same sound, the letter *t*. After all, then, and once the key was found, the complexities of hieroglyphic writing were really no worse than they are in modern English.

Jean-François's work indicated that phonetic writing had been in use in ancient Egypt as early as 3400 B.C. In their writing the Egyptians went to nature for signs to use as letters: birds, plants, animals and other symbols which baffled even the Greeks. The ancient Egyptians used these symbols, which were their form of our alphabet, in three ways: 1) as a whole word or root; 2) as a sound, of phonetic value; 3) to define pictorially the meaning of a word.

This ancient form of writing became the exclusive property of the temples, used by the priests for holy decrees and other holy purposes. A simpler form of the writing developed, or was invented deliberately, for everyday use. It was known as hieratic, which, in turn, gave way to the still simpler form of writing called demotic. The hieroglyphs were used by the priests until as late as the fourth century A.D., when paganism finally collapsed.

This information, once the hieroglyphs became readable, was borne out by a portion of the message inscribed on the Rosetta Stone:

> The priests have decreed that this decree shall be inscribed upon a stele of hard stone in the writing of the

divine words [hieroglyphs], and in the writing of the books [demotic], and in the writing of the Greeks.

Jean-François said that he hoped to discover in Egyptian writing the origins of the alphabets of Egypt's neighbors, for Egyptian writing may have been the model upon which the peoples of western Asia built their own alphabets. (In Germany about this time, George Grotefend, working with Sumerian cuneiform texts, was proving this supposition wrong.)

"Decipherment of the hieroglyphs would," Jean-François stated, "give us an accurate chronological view of Egypt. We would gain a knowledge of their religions, their institutions, and a huge part of lost history would live once again." It was a bold statement, but his belief has stood the test of time.

Jean-Francois's "letter" pointed a certain and sure route back to ancient Egypt. But when it was finally circulated in 1822, it caused an immediate uproar in academic circles in Paris, England and elsewhere. There were plenty of loud voices to deny this accomplishment, to belittle Jean-François for claiming to have found an alphabet in hieroglyphic symbols. In England, and in Germany to a less extent, he was scorned, his translations rejected. Few of these loud-voiced critics bothered to put his method to the test themselves on other inscriptions. There were those in England who cried "foul," claiming that credit for deciphering hieroglyphics rightly belonged to Dr. Young. These critics failed to see the absurdity of their own stand. They denied any validity in Jean-François's method and results and on

the other hand claimed success from them for Dr. Young!
The rivalry created in this manner, the desire of neither
Jean-François nor Dr. Young, continued for many years.

This bickering argument was a blot upon the bright page
of British Egyptology.

Jean-François worked on quietly, supported by those
scholars who were willing to attempt to verify his methods.
Successfully, he read all the royal names encircled by cartouches, and proceeded to create an Egyptian grammar and
a dictionary of hieroglyphics, which Jean-Jacques edited
for him. In 1824 his *Précis au système hiéroglyphique*
(Précis of the Hieroglyphic System) was published. Jean-
François knew that fame was his. As long as memory of ancient Egypt lasted, his name would live for bringing a lost
civilization back into the stream of human life.

Jean-Jacques and Zoë, who now had four children, were
overjoyed at Jean-François's success. Rosine, a little worried
by some of the vicious criticisms, realized more fully than
ever before that the man she had married was a most remarkable human being.

This same year, to his great delight, Jean-François's first
and only child was born, a girl. This daughter he gave the
Egyptian name of Zorai'de, and whenever he could be with
her he enjoyed playing with her, generally calling her his
"little spring flower." Zorai'de looked like her father, and
had the same dark complexion and slight tilt at the corner
of her eyes.

With the arrival of Zorai'de, the life of Jean-François
Champollion changed drastically. Louis XVIII, missed by
hardly anyone, died September 18, 1824, in Paris. He was

153

succeeded by his brother Charles X, and the fortunes of Jean-François took a decided turn for the better.

The year he ascended the throne, Charles X sent for Champollion. French scholars still had a great need for material from which to develop knowledge of ancient Egypt. In Italy, at Turin, Leghorn, Rome and Naples, the museums contained many relics from ancient Egypt. Jean-François's assignment was to tour these museums, delve into their archives and make copies of inscriptions and learn all he could from the relics.

At Turin, Jean-François made a sensational discovery! Up until this time, all that the scholars had that dealt with Egyptian burial practices was information gleaned from a work by Clemens of Alexandria, who lived about A.D. 200. It was really a small part of the works known to have been written by Clemens, but it was a vitally important book. This work, which Jean-François found in Turin, added more luster to his name. He called his find *Ritual*, but Richard Lepsius, the German scholar who eventually published this work, more correctly called the work *The Book of the Dead*. He commented that it was the only example of a great Egyptian literary work transmitted to us directly from the early pharaohs. What was more remarkable was that these works (for three have been found in Egyptian tombs of the XVIII Dynasty) were written in pure hieroglyphics. Most other examples of Egyptian literature that were then available were written in the hieratic script, the simplified form of hieroglyphs. Later *Books of the Dead* are also written in hieratic.

The Book of the Dead, when it was finally understood,

proved indeed to be one of the most vital documents ever discovered from ancient Egypt. It was incredible that it could have lain neglected for so long. Without this book much of the knowledge we have of ancient Egypt would still be shrouded in mystery. In deciphering the hieroglyphs, and now in discovering this book, Jean-François had finally torn away the veil that hid ancient Egypt from our view.

This important book contains nearly two hundred religious explanations, some of them dating far back into dynastic history. Some of the chapters deal with funeral rituals and customs and beliefs about life after death. One very significant section describes the doctrine of Osiris, a belief in resurrection and the experience of the *Ka* (soul) on its dangerous journey into the life of the next world. These rituals were, apparently, placed with the mummied dead, for they would need their instructions on the journey to the hereafter. There was an explanation of how the deceased had to make a confession to the god Thoth, who kept records of the dead. The beautifully illustrated book is written on papyrus. The original, which Jean-François discovered at Turin, contains 165 chapters and it is still kept at the museum.

Jean-François was kept very busy copying the inscriptions from *The Book of the Dead*. He was also making notes for himself because he planned to publish the texts with explanations of his own. Alas, when he had completed this laborious task, his own notes were mislaid. The proposed book was never written. Later, there was a report that an obscure researcher named Salvolini had stolen Jean-François's notes and used them himself.

Charles X was delighted with the skill and care that went into Champollion's detailed reports of his mission to Italy. On Jean-François's return in 1826, he appointed him Keeper of the Egyptian Collections of the Louvre. Jean-François had come a long way from the days when he occupied a shabby room near the great museum of which he had now become a director. He was gratified and happy to have this position which provided him peace and security in which to continue his researches into the civilization of ancient Egypt. He published more books, one on the Egyptian deities and one on the results of his research in Turin.

The results that accrued from the hectic years of 1821-1822 had provided a solid basis upon which to expand knowledge of the pharaohs and learn about the culture of ancient Egypt. Hieroglyphics, the "picture writing" of the Greek and Roman historians and travelers, was the oldest form of writing developed in Egypt. The demotic script appeared to have come into use about the fifth century B.C. It was employed by the priests of Isis until about A.D. 450.

These facts that now became known were almost a miracle in themselves. Many men, in following years, added to the store of interpretations of Egyptian texts. It is incredible that these men have been able to solve so many mysteries that hid a once mighty people for so many centuries. The Greeks themselves had a system of writing that was full of tricks. Sometimes they would write a first line from left to right and then the next line following would be from right to left, and so on until the message was completed.

Employing the system of values he had discovered, Jean-

François applied it to the list of over two hundred groups of signs that Dr. Thomas Young believed he had correctly deciphered. Of this list, Jean-François was able to prove that Dr. Young had been correct at least seventy-six times, a remarkable feat for a man who did not specialize in dead languages.

CHAPTER 11

EGYPT

Under Charles X it was forgotten that Jean-François had once been accused of being a traitor. The king held in high regard the young man he had appointed to the Louvre. In 1828, he again summoned Jean-François for an appointment. This new appointment was beyond his wildest dreams. When he left the presence of the king he felt as if he were in a daze, but it was a pleasant, rosy sort of feeling. He collected his wits and dashed off to his brother Jean-Jacques with the news.

"You look very pleased with yourself," Jean-Jacques said.

Jean-François replied, "You can never guess what has just happened to me!"

Zoë, observing his excitement, sat down to listen to the news.

"Then tell me," Jean-Jacques said.

"I am to lead an expedition to Egypt!"

"Oh, how perfectly wonderful for you, Sagîr!" Zoë exclaimed.

Jean-Jacques' mouth fell open, then he gulped. "You're to do what?"

"That's right," Jean-François said. "The king has appointed me to lead an expedition to Egypt! Never in my life did I think such a thing would happen to me! But I am a little worried, Jacques. Because there have been reports of fighting between Arabs and Turks in Egypt, there are those who advise that the expedition be put off. But it is precisely *because* of the reports of destruction that I feel we *must* go now! Who can tell what monuments might be destroyed and lost forever? I believe my view will prevail because the king is very interested."

"How very fortunate you are, Sagîr, but you deserve this chance." Somewhat wistfully Jean-Jacques added, "I wish I could accompany you. But I can't afford it and I must stay with Zoë and the children. Also, someone must watch over Rosine and Zorai'de while you are away."

"Of course, Sagîr, you know we will do our best to take care of Rosine and Zorai'de. How long do you think you will be gone?" Zoë asked.

"The expedition is being planned to last about eighteen months," Jean-François said.

"This news is more than good," Jean-Jacques said. "I shall have the chance to finish editing your work without your constant altering of details." He laughed. "By the time you get back, Sagîr, I shall be free of that and able to help you organize and prepare your reports on the trip."

"Actually," Jean-François said, "it's a kind of double expedition. You see, Leopold II, the Grand Duke of Tuscany, is also interested. He is financing and organizing a party under Ippolito Rosellini to travel with my group. They will soon be joining us in Paris to organize the details, but I am to be the leader of both groups."

It did not seem to make any difference to Rosine that her husband would be gone so long. She seldom saw much of him anyway. She saw even less of him during the busy days of interviewing and choosing the members of the expedition, planning dates and schedules. Zorai'de, catching fire from her father's excitement, followed him from room to room when he was in the house. Distracted though he was, Jean-François was patient with her and took the time to explain what all the excitement was about. Zorai'de, who was just a little over four years of age, was not an exceptional child in any way and she could not grasp anything except that her father was a very happy and excited man.

From the start, Jean-François was very popular with the men who were to accompany him on this expedition. They called him "the General" and themselves the "general staff." Jean-François watched out for their interests, and they formed a boisterous, happy group of young men about to begin the adventure of a lifetime.

Ippolito Rosellini, a native of Pisa and a professor of oriental languages, had much in common with Champollion. He was quite content to be second in command, and a mutual respect and warmth marked their relationship. Rosellini was twenty-eight years old, ten years younger than Jean-François, and their ability to work together bode well for the expedition.

Jean-François won over the pessimists who wanted to postpone the expedition, and on July 31, 1828, they sailed from France. As they neared Alexandria their ship was caught in a very bad storm. Some members of the party, fearing the ship was going to sink, wrote messages, which they put in bottles and tossed overboard. But the storm passed.

From the moment the yellow, palm-dotted coastline of Egypt came into view, Jean-François experienced the feeling that he was returning home. Once he set foot ashore, he was in a totally new world, yet one that somehow seemed familiar. The French consul-general was far from happy to see the expedition arrive in Alexandria. There had, indeed, been fighting and troubles in the country and he did not relish having to be responsible for this group of lighthearted young explorers.

Because of his mastery of their language, Jean-François was able to open many doors among important native people. He formed a friendship with Pasha Mehemed Ali, although he had mixed feelings about Mehemed Ali. The pasha entertained the party lavishly between excursions around Alexandria. But Jean-François soon learned that the pasha owned all the land that was worth anything, and he was shocked and dismayed by the contrast between the sumptuousness of the entertainment and hospitality the pasha provided for the expedition and his complete indifference to the dreadful poverty of his people. Jean-François was to learn that this kind of contrast was the rule, not the exception, in Turkish-ruled Egypt.

He was, however, thrilled by all he saw. He would have been even more thrilled had he known that, when archaeologists did finally take their spades and dig in the sand, more of ancient Egypt would be revealed than anybody then dreamed existed. All his party was able to do was study what ruins stood on the surface of the ground.

Soberly, one day, Jean-François remarked to Rosellini, "Everywhere I go, everywhere I look, everything I touch is like renewing acquaintance with things I have known and loved all my life."

"The feeling of wonderment touches us all," Rosellini replied, "yet I can readily understand the special quality it must have for you."

It was a happy group, filled with boundless enthusiasm, that wandered about the ruins on the outskirts of Alexandria. They had shaved their heads and covered them with enormous, bright-colored turbans. They dressed themselves in native pantaloons and bright brocade native jackets edged with gold braid. They completed their outfits by wearing bright yellow boots, much favored by rich Turks and Egyptians.

Jean-François dressed more soberly in native costume. To a man his companions swore that he appeared as though he had never worn any other type of clothing. He looked like a native-born Egyptian. As the party roamed about the ruins, sketching and measuring and copying inscriptions, swarms of natives followed them about. They were friendly people and took great delight in the outlandish costumes the explorers wore. Jean-François was particularly popular, for he spoke to them easily in their own tongue. Dancing about, laughing gaily, they would point him out to one another calling him "the man who could read stones!"

Jean-François's party did not remove anything from the ruins unless he decided no harm would be done. It distressed him deeply to find that in many instances Mehemed Ali had torn stones from ancient monuments and used them to build storage bins as well as his palaces!

In September, embarking on the *Isis*, one of the largest ships to sail on the Nile, they set out for Cairo. At Said, they found ruins vandalized and partially flooded. All along the way the signs of disease and poverty among the people continued to shock Jean-François and his companions. They reached Cairo on September 20 and were warmly welcomed and again offered lavish hospitality.

Traveling in Lower Egypt, the expedition paused at the site of the great pyramids at Gizeh. The huge sphinx which guards the approach to the pyramid of Cheops (Khufu) was then mostly covered with sand. They climbed the side of Cheops' pyramid to examine the large hole where, centuries earlier, grave robbers had broken into the pharaoh's tomb. Cheops had reigned 2900–2877 B.C. It was the ancient historian Herodotus who spelled the pharaoh's name Cheops instead of the Egyptian Khufu. Herodotus stated that Cheops had employed 100,000 men for twenty years in building his pyramid. From the top of the pyramid, in the far distance, they could see the site of Sakkara, toward which they were headed. The expedition continued up the river Nile, stopping at Memphis. They found the remains at Sakkara largely destroyed, having been plundered for building materials. Making up a caravan of camels, they explored about the area of Memphis. Everywhere he turned, Jean-François saw confirmation of hypotheses he had worked out years before. He identified buildings, assigned them to their correct place in time and their proper era in the long history of ancient Egypt. At Memphis, where King Ptolemy V, Epiphanes, had been deified as reported on the Rosetta Stone, Jean-François classified correctly architecture of different epochs by merely glancing over the ruins.

Moving on into Upper Egypt, at Abydos they examined dynastic sites as well as those dating from the Greco-Roman periods of Egyptian history. Almost every site they examined had known the ravage wrought by vandals. At Dendera were more sites from the dynastic period. Around the next bend in the river Nile was Naqada, with sites dating from predynastic times. Farther up the river lay Karnak, Luxor and Thebes, which was once the capital of ancient Egypt. The party, busy all the while sketching and copying, was staggered by what these ruins must once have been. For Jean-François, they still had life and movement, for his spirit was with the ancient Egyptians as they had lived.

They were anxious to move on up the river. While they were getting ready, the Turkish governor, Mohammed Bey, sent his son after them, insisting that they stay and be his guests!

Finally the governor let them continue their journey and they headed toward Thebes and the high point of their trip. Here they discovered a temple Cleopatra had built commemorating the birth of her son Cesarion. Though about Thebes, too, there had been fighting and the destruction Jean-François had been warned of in Paris, he was very glad the expedition had not been postponed. It was as if everything he had seen before had been but a prelude. There before him was a forest of gigantic sandstone columns, 134 of them arranged in sixteen rows. Twelve of them in the center stood sixty-four feet high and had circumferences of over thirty feet. The shafts were covered with reliefs and hieroglyphs.

The riches in front of his eyes, for as far as he could see were more pillars and figures of gods and goddesses, temples and courts, staggered the imagination. It would take many lifetimes to copy the inscriptions and translate them.

Jean-François wrote to friends in Paris, "At last I have visited the palace, or rather the city, of monuments, Karnak. I found there all the splendor of the pharaohs, all that those people planned and to a great extent executed. . . . No nation on earth, ancient or modern, has ever conceived architecture on so noble and vast a scale. . . . The Egyptians of old thought like men a hundred feet high."

At Edfu they discovered a well-preserved temple that had been constructed on much older foundations. Jean-François was very upset to discover that Mehemed Ali's new palace in Upper Egypt had been built with materials taken from the monuments of Amenhotep II and Thutmose III.

The weather turned very cold when they returned, near the end of December, from these sites to the river. At Abu Simbel two beautiful temples, enormous and covered with sculptures, were found. It proved very difficult to explore these beautiful buildings. Shifting sands had covered the entrances and it proved very difficult to remove it and keep it removed. At this point, too, at Aswan, the party turned around to journey back to Alexandria. The heat, and now the cold, took its toll on Jean-François, and more than once he was immobilized by attacks of gout.

All the places the expedition visited yielded information that confirmed the conclusions that Jean-François had made in Paris. At a site called Mit Rahina, the expedition discovered temples and a cemetery. At Sakkara, near the oldest dressed-stone structure in the world, the step pyramid of Zoser, Jean-François found the inscribed name of a pharaoh, Onnos.

At Dendera, Jean-François enjoyed a personal triumph that was, for him, the high point of the whole journey. He also suffered another attack of gout that kept him in bed while his party copied the many inscriptions they had found. Dendera was the site of the immense temple which had provoked so much controversy a few years before, making Jean-François the laughing stock of Paris. But the last laugh was to be his.

The inside of the temples were very hot, usually, and Jean-François found that, though the men were usually soaked with perspiration when they worked, the heat actually helped ease his pain. It proved so again at Dendera. As the expedition approached the site from the river, the landscape lay silver and black before them. There was an air of magic where bright moonlight-silhouetted features could be seen as brightly as in daylight. The air was crisp and very clear. About two miles distant, after they had scrambled ashore, they could see the stark outlines of the great temple. Above it, countless stars shone. The party gasped at the loveliness of the sight they beheld. "A fairy scene in the moonlight," one enchanted member of the group called it.

Chattering, laughing, singing songs to while away the time of the dusty trek to the temple's grounds, the group

scrambled through thorn scrub, through tall rough grass, until the temple rose before them. They had met no people until suddenly an old Arab rose before them, ragged and dirty, blocking their path. The Arab was extremely frightened by the sight of this garishly dressed group of Europeans who had so rudely awakened him. His first thought, he said after they had soothed him, was that he had died and awakened in the next world!

Finally, Jean-François and his party stood under the portico of the great temple. This building was the best-preserved structure they had found. Later, writing about his impressions, Jean-François described how the group had "sensed a perfect peace, and outside the dark entrance lay a world of incredible beauty, bathed in radiant moonlight as bright as day." Torches were lit and a rough examination was made of the interior. It was obvious there would be much work copying the many inscriptions here. Jean-François wrote a few words of his feelings at this first sight of the temple at Dendera:

> I will not try to describe the impression that the temple made on us. Separate parts can be measured, but it is impossible to give an idea of the whole structure. To the very highest degree, the temple blends majesty and grace. We stayed there two hours, filled with ecstasy, wandering through the halls, trying to read the outside inscriptions by the glittering moonlight.

This temple, because of what he had endured on its behalf in Paris, was of very special interest to Jean-François. When his notes and observations were completed, he had established that this temple was, indeed, a temple to the goddess of love and mirth, Hathor. Those who maintained it was a temple of Isis were wrong. Its age, too, he was able to establish. Kings from the New Kingdom, Thothmes III, Rameses the Great, and many others had added their work to the construction. Later, the Ptolemies and even Romans in the time of Trajan had put finishing touches to the immense, beautiful structure.

This temple was an architectural masterpiece, a tribute to the skill of the ancient Egyptian builders and designers. However, some of its sculptures and bas reliefs, Jean-François pointed out, "were the tasteless product of a later, decadent epoch, unworthy of the beauty of the building itself." At Dendera he found the inscribed name of Augustus Caesar. At the other controversial site, Esneh, he found the name of Antonius. Caesar and Anthony, then, *had* known both these places. Of the zodiacs reported by Napoleon's expedition, they found no trace.

All too soon the eighteen months in Egypt passed and Jean-François was sorry to leave. By December 23, 1829, they reached Toulon and headed for Paris. Jean-François was highly praised by his party for the concern and care for their well-being that he always showed. Paris, they found, was as politically restless as ever.

In 1830, the man who had opened the door to Egypt for Jean-François, Charles X, was forced to abdicate after ruling six years. Louis Philippe was offered the throne. This Louis, Duke of Chartres, had fought against the revolutionaries. An order for his arrest had been issued but he had escaped into Austria. He had spent the next few years wandering in foreign lands, but had returned to France with the restoration of the monarchy. Now he promised to be a constitutional king and took the throne.

Secure in his peaceful pursuit of his studies, Jean-François paid little heed to these changes other than to profoundly regret the abdication of Charles X, who had done so much for him.

The studies of Egypt that Jean-François had already published set the seal on his fame, but his major work was not yet completed. In 1831 his great talent was acknowledged in a manner that gave him a good deal of satisfaction. Jean-François was elected a member of the Academy of Inscriptions and was given the chair of Egyptian Antiquities, a post specially created for him by the Collège de France.

By this time, Jean-François's theories and methods had won many more adherents. Even so, there was no shortage of critics who did everything they could to discredit him. Nor, officially, were his theories yet accepted; this was a formality that had yet to appear. In England, particularly, his ideas and the proofs he offered were resisted beyond all common sense, and the obvious correctness of his translations of hieroglyphics was seriously questioned. Those who did not resist, since his work had given truth to some of Thomas Young's translations, still claimed vociferously that Young should be given credit for deciphering the hieroglyphic script. That such personal rancor can exist among men who were, otherwise, eager searchers for knowledge and truth is a human paradox.

Jean-François continued to ignore his detractors and worked steadily on his books, letting his work speak for itself. He was not, alas, destined to see his works published or to taste the final fruits of victory over prejudice. The sickness (perhaps pneumonia) that had attacked him in the early days in Paris had taken its toll of his strength. The heat of the desert in Egypt, the cold nights, the painful gout he had suffered also weakened him. In addition they had all had to cope with the plagues of flies in Egypt that spread filth and disease, swarming about their food before they could get it to their mouths. Highly strung, quickly active, the intense mental efforts he had been making since he was a boy of five years consumed his energy at a reckless rate.

On the last day of December 1831, Jean-François, forty-one years old, suffered a stroke. Quickly, Rosine sent for Zoë and Jean-Jacques. The attack left him partially paralyzed, but the doctors seemed to feel that he would recover. Consulting together, Rosine and Zoë and Jean-Jacques decided not to reveal that Jean-François was ill. Rosine was hopeful of her husband's recovery, but, on January 27, Jean-François was attacked by another, more severe stroke. This one robbed him of his speech, but his mind seemed unaffected. Again, hoping he would recover, the family decided not to make public Jean-François' condition.

Their secrecy helped create the impression that the great Egyptologist had died suddenly. On March 4, 1832, the academic world of Paris was shocked to learn that the brilliant young scholar was dead. The family had no desire to hide this news, but when the authorities suggested they perform an autopsy, they were refused. On March 6, at the Saint Roch Coptic Chapel, where he had worshiped for many years, a memorial service was held. Afterward, Jean-François was taken to the Père-Lachaise Cemetery in Paris, where he rests on the Avenue des Acacias.

Jean-François' premature death was an irrevocable loss to the science of Egyptology, which he had done so much to develop and nourish, and a great loss to fine scholarship in general. He had not lived long enough to see his theories and ideas officially accepted. But they *were* accepted and the way was open for other men to proceed with the rescue of ancient Egyptian civilization from the oblivion of millenia. As he predicted, this civilization would live again.

The story of Jean-François Champollion did not end with his death. From beyond the grave his thoughts and ideas, his theories and his results continued to build the fantastic story he had really begun as a child of four by teaching himself to read.

Eight-year-old Zorai'de could remember the tears and the mourning, but as she grew up she could recall little else about the great man who had been her father.

CHAPTER 12

THE TRIUMPH OF GOODWILL

In Figeac the name of the square near the birthplace of Jean-François was changed to the Place Champollion. A small obelisk surrounded by an iron fence was erected to his memory and another memorial was erected in the grounds of the Collège de France in Paris. This statue shows Jean-François deep in thought, his head resting on his left hand, his knee raised beneath his elbow as his foot is perched on the head of an Egyptian sphinx. The memorial is simply inscribed *Champollion le Jeune*.

After the death of Champollion, Sir Gardner Wilkinson, a British man of science and a gentleman, paid the following scrupulously fair tribute to the great French scholar:

> To have had frequent occasion to introduce the name of Champollion, to whom we are so deeply indebted, without paying a just tribute to his talents, is to me a reproach which I cannot suffer to remain unremoved. I do not wish to enter into the question respecting the discovery of the proper mode of reading the hieroglyphics: suffice it to say, that Dr. Young gave the first idea and proof of their alphabetical force,

which was even for some time doubted by Champollion. And the merit of originality in this point is due to our distinguished countryman, I can bear satisfactory testimony, having, with my friend Sir William Gell, as early as the summer of 1821, so far profited by Dr. Young's opinions on the subject as to be enabled to suggest the supposed value of two or three characters, beside those he had already ascertained; our taking this view of the question being solely in consequence of his discovery *that they were representative of letters*. But it remained for the genius of Champollion to kindle the spark thus obtained into a flame, and to display by its light, the path which led to a clear insight into the subject, to perfect the discovery, and to lay down certain rules, applicable in individual as well as in general cases; and in justice to him be it confessed that, if our knowledge of hieroglyphics were confined to the limited extent to which it was carried by Dr. Young, we should have no regular system to guide us in the interpretation of them, and should know little more than the alphabetic value of a few letters, without the means of affixing a positive construction to a single sentence on any Egyptian monument.

We cannot forgive the ungenerous conduct of those who, from private pique, summon up and misapply talents to pervert truth; denying the merit of labors, which every one acquainted with the subject, knows to have been crowned with unexampled and wonderful success. This is not an era when we could believe men capable of lending themselves to the unworthy office of maligning one no longer living to defend himself, and one who, present or absent, merits and possesses the respect and admiration of every unprejudiced person. Yet have some been found in more than one country, prompted to this malicious act by personal enmity, envy of his superior talents and success, or by that affectation of skepticism, which, while it endeavors to conceal ignorance, often hopes to acquire credit for discernment and superior knowledge.

When the subject of hieroglyphics becomes better understood, and the world is capable of judging how much we owe to him, the wonderful ingenuity of Champollion will be appreciated; and the greatest praise we can bestow on him is confidently to pronounce, that time will do justice to his merits, and experience prove the truth of what inexperience now calls in question.

Jean-François Champollion's *Egyptian Grammar* and *Dictionary of Hieroglyphics* finally saw publication in 1836, four years after his death. These works, edited by his brother, placed extremely valuable tools in the hands of Egyptologists.

The results of the expedition to Egypt were left to Ippolito Rosellini to publish, and the first volume appeared the year Jean-François died, 1832. The last of the ten volumes of this huge work appeared in 1840. All of this material was accepted and Jean-François' method of translation, his alphabet and dictionary began to be widely used.

In England, sadly, despite the words of Sir Gardner Wilkinson, there remained those who would not accept the indisputable evidence that was now available and could be checked. Many German Egyptologists, too, shared the view of these English colleagues, rejecting the works of Champollion. Happily, there were English and German scholars who found this attitude disgraceful. They carried on the fight for acceptance of the ideas of the great French Egyptologist.

For years this struggle continued. Then final vindication and support came in a most dramatic manner.

In 1866, the German Egyptologist Richard Lepsius found a stone in the ruins of San (Tanis) in the Nile Delta which bore the Decree of Canopus. This decree, like that found on the Rosetta Stone, was inscribed in hieroglyphics, demotic and Greek, and it was called the Decree of Canopus because it was inscribed there in 239 B.C.

(Canopus was the name of an ancient Egyptian seaport which stood at the western mouth of the river Nile. Many beautiful vases painted with hieroglyphics were found at the site. These contained the viscera of persons who had been embalmed and mummified. The lids of the jars were made in the shape of the head of the dead person and painted with his features.)

Using Jean-François's methods, a long and exhaustive study was conducted of the Decree of Canopus, inscribed in honor of Ptolemy III, Euergetes I, his queen, and their daughter. Jean-François' methods were completely vindicated, and study of the Decree of Canopus proved the accuracy of his grammar and his dictionary of hieroglyphics.

The dark blot on the page of British Egyptology was finally removed in 1896. Sir Peter le Page Renouf addressed the Royal Society in London. He paid homage to Jean-François, and when he finished his address Jean-François stood at the pinnacle where he belonged, *sixty-four years after his death!*

Archaeology began to develop at an ever-growing rate as more and more men took spades and dug about the tombs and ancient sites of Egypt. Egyptologists forged ahead with their translations of hieroglyphics. As their laws, rituals, literature, customs and manner of life became known, there emerged the picture of a people who had carried art and science to a height from which modern man has only recently begun to rise higher. Through the efforts, and often hardships, of archaeologists and Egyptologists a great gap in the astounding continuity of human life on this planet has been closed. Too, the ancient Egyptians, in many respects, have been shown to be men so much like ourselves that they might be our neighbors in time.

Thousands of years may pass, civilizations rise and fall, some disappear for thousands of years, but human nature changes very little, as is shown by Amonemhat's advice to his son when he should succeed his father as pharaoh:

> Hearken to that which I say to thee,
> That thou mayest be king of the earth,
> That thou mayest be ruler of the lands,
> That thou mayest increase good.
> Harden thyself against all subordinates.
> The people give heed to him who terrorizes them;
> Approach them not alone.
> Fill not thy heart with a brother,
> Know not a friend,
> Nor make for thyself intimates,
> Wherein there is no end.

177

When thou sleepest, guard for thyself thine own
     heart;
For a man has no people,
In the day of evil.
I gave to a beggar,
I nourished the orphan;
I admitted the insignificant,
As well as him who was of great account.
But he who ate my food made insurrection;
He to whom I gave my hand aroused fear therein.

A harsh doctrine, perhaps, but such was the price a man must pay when he became sole ruler of a vast kingdom.

Amonemhat, first king of the XII Dynasty, 2000 B.C., lived in troublesome times. Another scholar, in his study of the writings of a wise man of the period, found the following evidence that Egypt was passing through a period of great disquiet which must have been much like the period in which Jean-François Champollion himself lived. Iper-wer wrote:

> Increase still more the good things which you possess and stop worrying. Do what you feel inclined to do and what will give you pleasure. Enjoy yourself while you are here and don't worry until the end comes.
> Enjoy each day to the fullest. For be sure no one can take what he possesses with him, and no one who has passed on can return.

Astonishing discoveries have been made in Egypt and to the present time archaeologists are still exploring the relics of the pharaohs. Probably the most spectacular find ever made was that of the tomb of the boy king Tutankhamen. In 1922 Howard Carter was exploring about the site of the tomb of Rameses VI in the Valley of the Tombs of the Kings, near Thebes. Some weeks later when his colleague Lord Carnavon arrived from England, excavation began.

The archaeologists, feeling their way along as they cleared rubbish away from the stone, found a passage below the tomb of Rameses. Following this passage they came to a flight of sixteen stone steps leading down from the passage. At the end of these stone steps they came to a sealed entry. When this entry was finally opened and examined an incredible sight of treasure met the two men's wondering gaze. Unlike the majority of the royal tombs, this one had, apparently, escaped the grave robbers. But more astonishing sights were yet to come.

The tomb complex of Tutankhamen was found to consist of four rectangular chambers. These were the antechamber, the storeroom, the annex and the burial chamber. These rooms were found to contain objects of great beauty which had been buried with the king. They provided valuable testimony to the high skill of ancient Egyptian jewelers and furniture makers, and the richness that surrounded the pharaohs in their courts. There were finely designed couches, figures of gods and goddesses, beautiful ornaments and vases that had been placed in the tomb for the king's use in the afterlife.

The most incredible discovery of all was that of the sarcophagus of Tutankhamen in the burial chamber. This sarcophagus was surrounded by richly ornamented shrines and treasures of all kinds set there for the king. The coffin was taken to another place to be examined and this was soon seen to be the finest object ever found in all of Egypt. There were three coffins, set one inside the other like Chinese boxes. Both the outer coffins were elegantly carved and decorated with gold and glass inlay. The third, inner, coffin was found to be of solid gold.

The mummy inside the gold coffin was a fantastic sight. It was immediately apparent that this king was a very young man when he died. On the face of the mummy was an exquisite gold mask inset with precious stones in the likeness of Tutankhamen. There were gold sandals on the feet and gold ornaments covered the tips of the toes and fingers. The gold headdress bore the heads of a vulture and a cobra, the signs of sovereignty. It was established that Tutankhamen had died when he was about eighteen years old.

A good deal of knowledge was gained from the discovery of this tomb. Tutankhamen, the boy king, reigned about nine years from around the middle of the fourteenth century B.C. The walls of the rooms of the burial complex provided detailed evidence of the events of the dead pharaoh's life and times.

Early in 1965, Professor Walter Emery published the news of a fascinating discovery in Egypt. Dr. Emery, an archaeologist at London University, has spent many years probing the ruins of Egypt. In 1964, while exploring one of the oldest dressed-stone structures in the world, the step pyramid of Zoser (2780 B.C.), at Sakkara, Dr. Emery discovered a temple complex of connecting passages. It may be that he has found the tomb of Imhotep. Imhotep was reputedly a fine physician, architect, philosopher and served brilliantly as the pharaoh's chief minister. Imhotep appears to be, from what is known of him now, one of the world's first truly great men. If Dr. Emery's discovery is borne out as he continues his work, another vital part of the story of ancient Egypt will have been brought to light.

Jean-Jacques Champollion lived long enough to witness the glory of his younger brother's achievements flowering. For this, he had sacrificed his own name. When he closed his eyes for the last time, at the great age of eighty-nine, he knew his sacrifice had not been wasted.

BIBLIOGRAPHY

American Association of Museums. *Tutankamun Treasures.* Smithsonian Institution, Distributors, 1961–1963.

Budge, E. A. Wallis. *Cleopatra's Needles & Other Egyptian Obelisks.* London: The Religious Tract Society, 1926.

Calder, Ritchie. *After the Seventh Day.* New York: Simon and Schuster, Inc., 1961.

Carrington, Richard. *A Million Years of Man.* Cleveland: The World Publishing Company, 1963.

Christophe, Robert. *The Executioners.* London: Arthur Barker, Ltd., 1961.

Edwards, I. E. S. *The Pyramids of Egypt.* Baltimore: Penguin Books, 1961.

Fairservis, Walter A., Jr. *The Ancient Kingdoms of the Nile and the Doomed Monuments of Nubia.* New York: Thomas Y. Crowell Company, 1962.

Hartleben, Hermine. *Champollion: Sein Leben und Sein Werk.* Berlin: Wideman, 1906.

Hawkes, Francis L. *The Monuments of Egypt.* New York: G. P. Putnam's Sons, 1849.

Keller, Werner. *The Bible as History.* New York: William Morrow & Company, 1956.

Markham, Felix. *Napoleon.* New York: New American Library, 1963.

Moffett, Cleveland. *The Reign of Terror.* New York: Ballantine Books, Inc., 1962.

Montet, Pierre. *Eternal Egypt.* New York: New American Library, 1964.

Mossiker, Frances. *Napoleon & Josephine.* New York: Simon and Schuster, Inc., 1964.

BIBLIOGRAPHY

Ober, J. Hambleton. *Writing: Man's Great Invention*. Baltimore: Peabody Institute Publication, 1965.

Palmer, R. R., ed. *Atlas of World History*. New York: Rand McNally & Company, 1957.

White, Anne Terry. *Lost Worlds: The Romance of Archaeology*. New York: Random House, Inc., 1941.

Woolley, Leonard, and Benn, Ernest. *Digging Up the Past*. Baltimore: Pelican Books, 1937.

INDEX

THE AUTHOR OF THIS BOOK

ALAN HONOUR, now a citizen of the United States and a resident of Richmond, Indiana, was born in London, England, in 1918, and was educated there. A veteran traveler, Mr. Honour spent seven years in the Royal Air Force during World War II, a tour of duty which took him throughout Africa and the Middle East. He once hitchhiked from Ismailia, Egypt, to Iran, by way of Palestine, Syria and Iraq. Writing assignments on film scripts in France and Italy occupied the years immediately after the war.

Since coming to the United States Mr. Honour has turned his attention to literature for young people. His previous books, *Cave of Riches, Ten Miles High, Two Miles Deep, The Unlikely Hero* and *Secrets of Minos*, have been very popular here. The latter has been twice honored. It was chosen as an Honor Book by the New York *Herald Tribune* and was selected as the "most distinguished work of literature for young adults published by an Indiana author in 1961" by the Indiana University Writer's Conference. All of Mr. Honour's books have appeared in translation abroad. He is a member of the Author's Guild and is listed in the British *Author's and Writer's Who's Who*.

THE MAN WHO COULD READ STONES *(Hawthorn, 1966)* was completely manufactured by American Book–Stratford Press of New York City. The body type is Linotype Janson, based on the letters of Anton Janson, a Dutch punchcutter who worked between 1660 and 1687.

A HAWTHORN BOOK